I0009741

Disclaimer

The publisher of this book is by no way associated with the National Institute of Standards and Technology (NIST). The NIST did not publish this book. It was published by 50 page publications under the public domain license.

50 Page Publications.

Book Title: Border Gateway Protocol Security

Book Author: David R. Kuhn; Kotikalapudi Sriram; Douglas C. Montgomery

Book Abstract: This document introduces the Border Gateway Protocol (BGP), explains its importance to the internet, and provides a set of best practices that can help in protecting BGP. Best practices described here are intended to be implementable on nearly all currently available BGP routers. While a number of enhanced protocols for BGP have been proposed, these generally require substantial changes to the protocol and may not interoperate with current BGP implementations. To improve the security of BGP routers, the recommendations listed below are introduced. While the recommendations can contribute to greatly improved BGP security, they are not a complete defense against all threats. Security administrators and decision makers should select and apply these methods based on their unique needs.

Citation: NIST SP - 800-54

Keyword: BGP; Border Gateway Protocol; computer security; routers

NIST

National Institute of
Standards and Technology
Technology Administration
U.S. Department of Commerce

Special Publication 800-54
July 2007

Border Gateway Protocol Security

Recommendations of the National Institute of Standards and Technology

Rick Kuhn
Kotikalapudi Sriram
Doug Montgomery

NIST Special Publication 800-54

C O M P U T E R   S E C U R I T Y

Computer Security Division
Information Technology Laboratory
National Institute of Standards and Technology
Gaithersburg, MD 20899-8930

July 2007

U.S. Department of Commerce

Carlos M. Gutierrez, Secretary

Technology Administration

Robert C. Cresanti, Under Secretary of Commerce for Technology

National Institute of Standards and Technology

William Jeffrey, Director

Reports on Computer Systems Technology

The Information Technology Laboratory TL) at the National Institute of Standards and Technology (NIST) promotes the U.S. economy and public welfare by providing technical leadership for the Nation's measurement and standards infrastructure. ITL develops tests, test methods, reference data, proof of concept implementations, and technical analyses to advance the development and productive use of information technology. ITL's responsibilities include the development of technical, physical, administrative, and management standards and guidelines for the cost-effective security and privacy of sensitive unclassified information in Federal computer systems. This Special Publication 800-series reports on ITL's research, guidance, and outreach efforts in computer security, and its collaborative activities with industry, government, and academic organizations.

National Institute of Standards and Technology Special Publication 800-54
Natl. Inst. Stand. Technol. Spec. Publ. 800-54, 61 pages (July 2007)

Note to Readers

This document is a publication of the National Institute of Standards and Technology (NIST) and is not subject to U.S. copyright. Certain commercial entities, equipment, or materials may be identified in this document in order to describe an experimental procedure or concept adequately. Such identification is not intended to imply recommendation or endorsement by the National Institute of Standards and Technology, nor is it intended to imply that the entities, materials, or equipment are necessarily the best available for the purpose.

For questions or comments on this document, contact Rick Kuhn, kuhn@nist.gov or 301-975-3337.

Acknowledgements

The authors (Rick Kuhn, Kotikalapudi Sriram, and Doug Montgomery) wish to thank their colleagues who reviewed drafts of this document and contributed its development. The authors also gratefully acknowledge and appreciate the many contributions from the public and private sectors whose thoughtful and constructive comments improved the quality and accuracy of this publication, including Tim Grance, Okhee Kim, Oliver Borchert, Sandy Murphy, Karen Scarfone, Stephen Hamilton, Brian McNamara, Patrik Fältström, Bruce Potter, Hank Nussbacher, Paul Ferguson, Peiter Zatko, Valdis Kletnicks, Hank Kilmer, Terry L. Sherald, Jack Harris, Janell Poindexter, and Lovell King II.

Certain commercial entities, equipment, or materials may be identified in this document in order to describe an experimental procedure or concept adequately. Such identification is not intended to imply recommendation or endorsement by the National Institute of Standards and Technology, nor is it intended to imply that the entities, materials, or equipment are necessarily the best available for the purpose.

Table of Contents

List of Appendices

List of Figures

List of Tables

4

This document introduces the Border Gateway Protocol (BGP), explains its importance to the Internet, and provides a set of best practices that can help in protecting BGP. Best practices described here are intended to be implementable on nearly all currently available BGP routers. While a number of enhanced protocols for BGP have been proposed, these generally require substantial changes to the protocol and may not interoperate with current BGP implementations. While the recommendations in this documentcan contribute to greatly improved BGP security, they are not a complete defense against all threats. Security administrators and decision makers should select and apply these methods based on their unique needs. To improve the security of BGP routers, the recommendations listed below are introduced.

Establish and use access control lists. This feature is available on nearly all routers. (See Section 4.2)

Use BGP graceful restart, when available with latest manufacturer-recommended default settings (see Section 5.1).

Use BGP peer authentication. Authentication is one of the strongest mechanisms for preventing malicious activity. Use Internet Protocol Security (IPsec) or BGP MD5 authentication mechanisms, if available (see Section 4.5 and Section 4.6).

Use prefix limits to avoid filling router tables. Routers should be configured to disable or terminate a BGP peering session and issue warning messages to administrators when a neighbor sends in excess of a preset number of prefixes. (see Section 4.2)

Only allow peers to connect to port 179. The standard port for receiving BGP session OPENs is port 179, so attempts by peers to reach other ports are likely to indicate faulty configuration or potential malicious activity.

Configure BGP to allow announcing only designated netblocks. This option will prevent the router from inadvertently providing transit to networks not listed by the autonomous system (AS) (see Section 2.3).

Filter all bogon prefixes. These prefixes (see Section 4.2.2) are invalid, so they should not appear in routes. Filtering them reduces load and helps reduce the ability of attackers to use forged addresses in denial of service or other attacks.

Where feasible, routers should do ingress filtering on peers (see Section 4.2, including 4.2.5).

Do not allow over-specific prefixes. Requiring routers to maintain large numbers of very specific prefixes can place excessive load on system resources. Recommendations vary as to what prefixes should be considered "over-specific", but a reasonable criterion could be those with prefix addresses in the range of /24 to /30.

Turn off fast external failover to avoid major route changes due to transient failures of peers to send keepalives. The "fast external failover" feature was designed to allow rapid failover to an alternate system when a link goes down. Without this feature, failover would not occur until BGP keepalive timers would permit recognition that the line had failed. It is not uncommon for lines to drop BGP sessions and then return, referred to as route flapping (see Section 3.2.4). Frequent flapping can trigger flap damping in upstream peers. Due to fast external failovers, flap damping would occur at upstream routers, which in turn results in prolonged peer-prefix unreachability and system instability. So turning off fast external failover normally represents a positive tradeoff in today's Internet.

Tradeoffs are involved with route flap damping (RFD), and current research suggests that it contributes to a number of problems. It should not be enabled unless the organization has a strong case for its use. See Section 3.2.4 for a discussion of RFD.

If route flap damping is used, longer prefixes should be damped more aggressively. Longer prefixes tend to be less stable, so longer RFD times are preferable. Sample half-time periods of RFD decay are as follows:

— less than /21 – manufacturer recommendation (conventional default is 15 minutes)

— /21 and shorter prefixes – not more than 30 minutes

— /22 to /23 prefixes – not more than 45 minutes

— /24 and greater prefixes – not more than 60 minutes.

Do not use route flap damping for netblocks that contain domain name system (DNS) root servers. These networks are normally the most stable, and can be expected to remain operating in all but the most exceptional circumstances. Damping these netblocks would therefore be likely to have more negative results than benefits. DNS root servers are also critical for Internet operations, so degraded access to them could cause widespread disruption of network operations.

Use soft reconfiguration, where practical. Normally a change in policy requires BGP sessions to be cleared before the new policy can be initiated, resulting in a need to rebuild sessions with consequent impact on routing performance. Thus, spoofed policy changes could be used for a denial of service attack, even if the policy changes themselves do not violate AS rules. Soft reconfiguration allows new policies to be initiated without resetting sessions. It is done on a per-peer basis, and can be set up for either inbound or outbound or both (for updates from and to neighbors, respectively). A recent improvement to soft reconfiguration is Route Refresh (RFC 2918 [36]). The route refresh capability allows dynamic exchange of route refresh requests between BGP peers, to obtain a re-advertisement of Adj-RIB-Out. This capability avoids the need to store unmodified copies of the routes learned from peers at all times.

Record peer changes. Log whenever a peer enters or leaves Established state, providing useful records for debugging or audit trails for investigating possible security problems.

1. Introduction

Although not well known among everyday users, the Border Gateway Protocol (BGP) is one of the critical infrastructure protocols for the Internet. BGP is a routing protocol, whose purpose is to keep systems on the Internet up to date with information needed to receive and transmit traffic correctly. Sending and receiving email, viewing Web sites, and performing other Internet activities require the transmission of messages referred to as packets. Packets sent on the Internet contain source and destination addresses, much like paper mail sent in envelopes. But packets do not go directly from a user's computer to their destination. Many intermediate systems may be involved in the transmission, and because there are many paths from one point to another, not all packets follow the same path between source and destination. The systems that packets pass through from one point to another all need to know where to forward a packet, based on the destination address and information contained in a routing table. The routing table says, for example, that packets with a destination of A can be sent to system H, which will then forward the packets to their destination, possibly through other intermediate nodes. (Note that the terms "routing table" and "forwarding table" are often used interchangeably, although technically the forwarding table is used to determine where packets will be sent. More on the distinction between these tables can be found in Section 2.1.) Because the Internet changes continuously, as systems fail or are replaced or new systems are added, routing tables must be updated constantly. BGP is the protocol that serves this purpose for the global Internet. When BGP fails, portions of the Internet may become unusable for a period of time ranging from minutes to hours.

Most of the risk to BGP comes from accidental failures, but there is also a significant risk that attackers could disable parts or all of network, disrupting communications, commerce, and possibly putting lives and property in danger. This document discusses the structure and function of BGP, potential attacks, available countermeasures, and the costs and benefits related to countermeasures. The emphasis in this publication is on measures that may be applied either immediately or in a short time. A variety of proposals have been introduced in standards bodies for more comprehensive approaches to BGP security, but issues are not yet settled as to which, if any, of these proposals will be adopted by the producers and consumers of routing equipment. The aim of this document is to give decision makers a selection of measures that can be deployed rapidly, yet provide significant improvements to routing security.

1.1 Authority

The National Institute of Standards and Technology (NIST) developed this document in furtherance of its statutory responsibilities under the Federal Information Security Management Act (FISMA) of 2002, Public Law 107-347.

NIST is responsible for developing standards and guidelines, including minimum requirements, for providing adequate information security for all agency operations and assets, but such standards and guidelines shall not apply to national security systems. This guideline is consistent with the requirements of the Office of Management and Budget (OMB) Circular A-130, Section 8b(3), "Securing Agency Information Systems," as analyzed in A-130, Appendix IV: Analysis of Key Sections. Supplemental information is provided in A-130, Appendix III.

This guideline has been prepared for use by Federal agencies. It may be used by nongovernmental organizations on a voluntary basis and is not subject to copyright, though attribution is desired.

Nothing in this document should be taken to contradict standards and guidelines made mandatory and binding on Federal agencies by the Secretary of Commerce under statutory authority, nor should these guidelines be interpreted as altering or superseding the existing authorities of the Secretary of Commerce, Director of the OMB, or any other Federal official.

1.2 Document Scope and Purpose

The purpose of this document is to provide agencies with background information on the Border Gateway Protocol and methods available for improving its security. Agencies are encouraged to tailor the recommended guidelines and solutions to meet their specific security or business requirements. Many extensions to BGP have been proposed, and a few have begun to see a degree of acceptance in the market. Because the aim of this document is to provide information on BGP as it is implemented for most systems, a number of extensions are out of scope, including several proposed modified BGP protocols for security, and multicast BGP. If these proposals begin to see widespread adoption, they may be included in a future draft of this publication.

1.3 Audience and Assumptions

This document assumes that the readers have some minimal operating system, networking, and security expertise. Because of the constantly changing nature of the information technology industry, readers are strongly encouraged to take advantage of other resources (including those listed in this document) for more current and detailed information.

1.4 Document   Organization

The document is divided into five sections followed by references. Because BGP may be unfamiliar to many readers, the next section explains the BGP protocol and its use in networking. Section 3.2 reviews potential attacks against BGP and lists countermeasures for each attack type. The countermeasures are explained in more detail in Section 4, followed by a collection of references for extensive information on the subjects covered in this document.

2. Border Gateway Protocol Overview

Although unknown to most users, the Border Gateway Protocol (BGP) is critical to keeping the Internet running. BGP is a routing protocol, which means that it is used to update routing information between major systems. BGP is in fact the primary interdomain routing protocol, and has been in use since the commercialization of the Internet. Because systems connected to the Internet change constantly, the most efficient paths between systems must be updated on a regular basis. Otherwise, communications would quickly slow down or stop. Without BGP, email, Web page transmissions, and other Internet communications would not reach their intended destinations. Securing BGP against attacks by intruders is thus critical to keeping the Internet running smoothly.

Many organizations do not need to operate BGP routers because they use Internet service providers (ISP) that take care of these management functions. But larger organizations with large networks have routers that run BGP and other routing protocols. The collection of routers, computers, and other components within a single administrative domain is known as an autonomous system (AS). An ISP typically represents a single AS. In some cases, corporate networks tied to the ISP may also be part of the ISP's AS, even though some aspects of their administration are not under the control of the ISP.

2.1 Review of Router Operation

In a small local area network (LAN), data packets are sent across the wire, typically using Ethernet hardware, and all hosts on the network see the transmitted packets. Packets addressed to a host are received and processed, while all others are ignored. Once networks grow beyond a few hosts, though, communication must occur in a more organized manner. Routers perform the task of communicating packets among individual LANs or larger networks of hosts.

To make internetworking possible, routers must accomplish these primary functions:

Parsing address information in received packets

Forwarding packets to other parts of the network, sometimes filtering out packets that should not be forwarded

Maintaining tables of address information for routing packets.

BGP is used in updating routing tables, which are essential in assuring the correct operation of networks. BGP is a dynamic routing scheme—it updates routing information based on packets that are continually exchanged between BGP routers on the Internet. Routing information received from other BGP routers (often called "BGP speakers") is accumulated in a *routing table*. The routing process uses this routing information, plus local policy rules, to determine routes to various network destinations. These routes are then installed in the router's *forwarding table*. The forwarding table is actually used in determining how to forward packets, although the term routing table is often used to describe this function (particularly in documentation for home networking routers).

2.2 Review of IP Addressing Notation

In the protocol used throughout today's Internet, IP version 4, IP addresses are made up of four bytes (8-bit fields, sometimes called octets), separated by periods, giving a total of 2^{32} addresses. Throughout this document, IP address blocks are given in the Classless Interdomain Routing (CIDR) format, A/n, where A is an IP address and n is the prefix length. That is, a block of addresses is indicated by giving the IP address prefix, followed by the number of bits (in decimal) used to designate the block. For example, NIST's IP addresses are in the range 129.6.0.0/16 Thus, NIST's address block of 129.6.0.0/16 indicates that any IP address beginning with "129.6" (addresses between the range 129.6.0.0 - 129.6.255.255) belongs to NIST. In other words, anything after the leftmost 16 bits can be used in combination with the leftmost 16 bits to designate an IP address for the NIST network. In binary, 129.6.0.0 is 1000 0001 0000 0110 0000 0000 0000 0000, so if the address block were given as 129.6.0.0/15, then anything after the first 15 bits would be available, so the range would be 129.6.0.0 – 129.7.255.255, because the second byte could be either 0000 0110 (decimal 6) or 0000 0111 (decimal 7). The size of an address block A/n is 2^{32-n}. For example, 129.6.0.0/16 is of size $2^{32-16} = 2^{16} = 65,536$, so NIST has 65,536 possible addresses.

The significance of address block sizes for routing is that more specific addresses are normally more efficient because more specific addresses specify a smaller block of addresses. For example, just as if we are sending a package from Los Angeles to Baltimore, it is better to use a truck going to Maryland than one that we only know is going somewhere on the East Coast. A "$/m$" block is 2^{n-m} times as large as a more specific $/n$ block ($m<n$). For example, suppose one router advertises that it can reach addresses in the range 129.6.0.0/16, and another announces 129.6.2.0/23. If an address of 129.6.3.164 is sent, the second router would normally be preferred, because the /16 address space is $2^7 = 128$ times as large as the /23 space ($2^{23} = 2^{16} \times 2^7$). This is one reason why routers are configured to give preference to the most specific addresses. Normally this practice makes routing more efficient, but when overly specific addresses are announced by mistake, routers can be overloaded (see for example Section 3.2.5).

2.3 How BGP Works

A set of computers and routers under a single administration, such as a university or company network, is known as an *autonomous system (AS)*. AS numbers are managed by the Internet Corporation for Assigned Names and Numbers (ICANN), a non-profit organization established by the U.S. Department of Commerce, which authorizes Internet registration organizations to assign AS numbers. As of May 2007, the Internet included more than 25,000 advertised ASes [20]. Packets that make up an Internet transmission, such as a request for a Web page, are passed from one autonomous system to another until they reach their destination. BGP's task is to maintain lists of efficient paths between ASes. The paths must be as short as possible, and must be loop-free. BGP routers exchange and store tables of reachability data, which are lists of AS numbers that can be used to reach a particular destination network. Figure 2-1 reflects the growth of BGP routing tables from 1989 – 2007. Active BGP entries (i.e., the number of reachable prefixes) in the Forwarding Information Base (FIB) table are currently approaching 300,000. The reachability information sent between ASes is used by each AS to construct graphs of Internet paths that are loop-free and as short as practical.

Each AS will have many routers for internal communication, and one or more routers for communications outside the local network. Internal routers use internal BGP (iBGP) to communicate with each other, and external routers use external BGP (eBGP). (iBGP and eBGP are the same protocol, but use different routing rules; iBGP does not advertise third-party, outside routes.) Any two routers that have established a connection for exchanging BGP information are referred to as *peers*. BGP peers use TCP, the same protocol used for email and Web page transmissions, to exchange routing information in the form of address prefixes that the routers know how to reach, plus additional data used in choosing among available routes. When a BGP router starts, it attempts to establish sessions with its configured peer routers by opening connections to port 179, the standard (or "well known") BGP port. The router attempting to establish the connection receives packets on a random port number greater than 1024 (referred to as an *ephemeral port*).

Autonomous systems can be categorized as either transit or non-transit. A *transit AS* is one with connections to multiple peer ASes, which will pass transit traffic between ASes. Large Internet service providers typically function as transit ASes. In most cases it will be easier to secure a *non-transit AS* because it is connected to only one neighbor AS. A transit AS, with multiple connections, can be more easily attacked and may require greater care in establishing filtering rules. However, a non-transit AS must ensure that it is not inadvertently being used for transit. This can be done by configuring BGP to announce only those networks that the AS specifically lists, and denying all others.

Initially, BGP peers exchange their full routing tables. After that, incremental updates are exchanged as routing configurations change. Conceptually, each BGP router uses three tables, or routing information bases (RIBs):

adj-RIB-In – routes learned from inbound update messages from BGP peers

loc-RIB – routes selected from the adj-RIB-In table

adj-RIB-Out – routes that the BGP router will advertise, based on its local policy, to its peers.

In actual operation, these tables may not be physically present. Their function should be supported, but how this functionality is implemented is a design decision for developers.

As shown in Figure 2-1, routing table entries have grown at a dramatic rate as the Internet achieved commercial use, and are projected to grow more rapidly in the future [17][21]. The presence of more entries in the routing tables causes more BGP updates to be propagated. In addition to routing table updates, KEEPALIVE packets are sent to maintain the connections between peers, in addition to special packets for various error conditions.

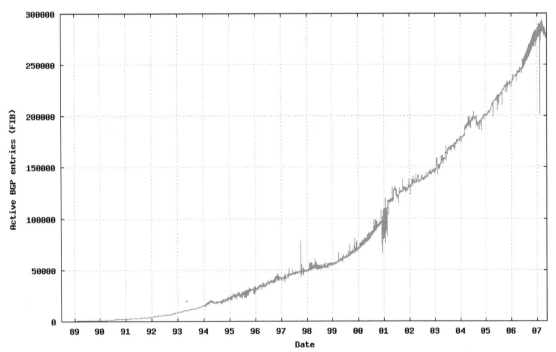

Figure 2-1. Growth of BGP Routing Tables, 1989 – 2007.

BGP messages are at least 19 bytes (8-bit bytes) and no longer than 4096 bytes. The BGP standard defines four message types:

OPEN

UPDATE

NOTIFICATION

KEEPALIVE.

BGP messages are sent over the TCP transport protocol. Once a TCP connection is established, a BGP OPEN message is sent. If the receiver accepts the OPEN, it returns a KEEPALIVE to acknowledge receipt of the OPEN. After that, UPDATE, KEEPALIVE, and NOTIFICATION messages are exchanged according to the needs of the two BGP peers. Appendix D shows the state transitions and message processing for BGP.

A common header is a prefix of all BGP messages. Table 2-1 shows the common header fields and field lengths.

Table 2-1. Common Header and Message Format

Field	Length (bytes)
Marker 16	
Length 2	
Type 1	
Message 0..4077 bytes	

OPEN messages contain values indicating the BGP version number, originating system's AS number, the "hold time" (which specifies the maximum time to wait before assuming a connection is down), sender's IP address, and optional parameters that may include authentication information. Table 2-2 shows the fields and field lengths for OPEN messages.

Table 2-2. OPEN Message Format

Field	Length (bytes)
BGP version	1
Autonomous system number	2
Hold time	2
BGP identifier (IP address)	4
Optional parameters length	1
Optional parameters	variable: 0..255 bytes

UPDATE messages do the real work of BGP: transferring routing information between BGP peers. This information is used by each AS to construct a routing graph that describes relationships between the autonomous systems. Each UPDATE message advertises a single route to a prefix (destination), or withdraws one or more unfeasible routes from service. Routes are described by one or more path attributes. A path attribute is a variable length triple <attribute type, attribute length, attribute value>. The next section describes path attributes and their potential values. Table 2-3 shows the fields in an UPDATE message.

Table 2-3. UPDATE Message Format

Field	Length (bytes)
Withdrawn routes length	2
Withdrawn routes	variable
Path attributes length	2
Path attributes <type, length, value>	variable
Network layer reachability information	variable

KEEPALIVE messages are exchanged between peers to indicate that the peers are up and running. KEEPALIVE messages are normally sent at an interval of one-third of the Hold Time parameter contained in the OPEN message that opened the connection. Table 2-4 shows the fields in a KEEPALIVE message.

Table 2-4. KEEPALIVE Message Format

Field	Length (bytes)
Marker	6
Length	2
Type	1

NOTIFICATION messages are sent to indicate various error conditions. Table 2-5 shows the fields in these messages.

Table 2-5. NOTIFICATION Message Format

Field	Length (bytes)
Error code	1
Error subcode	1
Length	2
Data	Variable

2.3.1 Path   Attributes

BGP uses what is known as a path vector algorithm to develop routing information. BGP update messages provide path information about entire sequences of routers for each destination. The data, or *path attributes*, are stored in the routing information base (RIB) of each BGP peer. Path attributes can be divided into the following categories:

Well-known mandatory

Well-known discretionary

Optional transitive

Optional non-transitive.

Well-known attributes are required to be processed by all BGP implementations. *Mandatory attributes* must be included in all UPDATE messages, while inclusion of *discretionary attributes* in UPDATEs is optional. Well-known attributes also must be forwarded to BGP peers, although they may be updated first. Important mandatory path attributes include ORIGIN, AS_PATH, and NEXT_HOP.

Path updates may also include *optional attributes*, which may not be supported by all BGP implementations. Because an implementation may not recognize some optional attributes, a *transitive* bit is used to distinguish those that must be passed along to other BGP peers.

ORIGIN is a well-known mandatory attribute. The ORIGIN attribute is set by the AS that originates the associated routing information. It is included in UPDATE messages of BGP speakers that propagate this information to their BGP peers.

AS_PATH is used for preventing loops by having each AS check for its AS number in AS_PATHs sent from other systems. Requirements for AS_PATH handling are as follows (see RFC 4271 [43]):

> After receiving a route in an UPDATE message, a BGP peer propagates it to other BGP speakers, after first modifying the route's AS_PATH according to the location of the destination BGP router.

> 1. AS_PATH associated with a route being advertised is not modified when the route is being advertised to another BGP speaker within the same AS.

> 2. If a route is being advertised to a BGP speaker in a neighboring AS, then the advertising BGP peer updates AS_PATH according to the following rules:

>> a. If the initial segment of AS_PATH is an AS_SEQUENCE attribute, then the local system prepends its own AS number in the leftmost position

>> b. If the initial segment of AS_PATH is an AS_SET attribute (indicating more than one AS reachable through this path), then the local system prepends a new path segment of type AS_SEQUENCE, that includes the speaker's own AS number.

> If a BGP speaker originates a route, then:

> 1. The originating BGP peer includes its own AS number in the AS_PATH attribute of UPDATE messages that are sent to neighboring ASes.

> 2. The originating BGP peer includes an empty AS_PATH attribute in all UPDATE messages sent to BGP speakers within the originating speaker's AS.

NEXT_HOP is maintained as the IP address of the first router in a neighboring AS. Each time a BGP route advertisement is received, NEXT_HOP is set to the IP address of the sending router if and only if an autonomous system boundary has been crossed. That is, if the message is received from another router within an AS, NEXT_HOP is not changed; it is updated only when a boundary router receives the advertisement from another AS.

The **MULTI_EXIT_DISC** (**multi-exit discriminator [MED]**) attribute is used to influence the entry point to a neighboring used when there are multiple connections with the AS. It is essentially a priority number, with lower MED values having preference. Because it is only relevant between neighboring peer ASes, the MED attribute is only propagated to neighboring ASes.

LOCAL_PREF is an attribute used within a single AS to influence exit points to remote destinations. LOCAL_PREF is a degree of preference for an external route, with higher numbers being preferred. Procedures for assigning this attribute are left open to individual interpretations by administrators.

2.3.2 Finding Paths – the BGP Decision Algorithm

Traffic in a network can be divided into two categories: local traffic, to be delivered within the AS; and transit traffic, which is received from outside the AS and is intended to pass through the AS and be passed off to another external AS. Routers use the information gained from BGP exchanges to determine how to route traffic destined for outside the network.

The BGP standard specifies that the choice between routes be based on "preconfigured policy information", but allows great flexibility in how the policy information is used for route selection. Typical considerations in route selection include the following:

- Do not consider IBGP path if not synchronized

- Do not consider path if no route to next hop

- Highest weight (local to router)

- Highest local preference (global within AS)

- Shortest AS path

- Lowest origin code IBGP < EBGP < incomplete

- Lowest MED

- Prefer EBGP path over IBGP path

- Path with shortest next-hop metric wins

- Lowest router-id.

The BGP decision procedure applies the routing information in three steps:

1. A preference number is calculated for each of the routes received from BGP peers in other ASes. Preferred routes are then advertised to other BGP speakers within the AS.

2. The router determines the best route for each destination from the preference levels received, then updates the local routing information base (RIB).

3. Routes in the RIB are sent to neighboring BGP peers in other ASes.

Figure 2-2 shows example routing table entries for paths to NIST's 129.6.0.0/16 addresses. Nine routes are available. Route #5 can reach the NIST address through 64.200.86.153 from 216.66.23.99. The cost metric for this route (100) is lower than other routes, so it is identified as the best route to the NIST system. Note that 100 is the inter-AS metric for this path; a second metric is listed for the interior gateway protocol (IGP). (IGP is a generic term for routing protocols used within (not between) ASes.)

```
                    BGP routing table entry for 129.6.0.0/16, version 8302807
Paths: (9 available, best #5)
  Advertised to non peer-group peers:
    64.62.142.154 64.71.128.254 128.223.60.102 128.223.60.103 128.223.60.108
    206.223.137.126 206.223.137.254 209.51.163.34 216.66.3.10 216.218.185.238
  6453 UUNET/ALTERNET (701) 49
    63.243.149.105 from 63.243.149.105 (207.45.223.13)
      Origin IGP, metric 48, localpref 100, valid, external
      Community: 6939:2000
  6453 UUNET/ALTERNET (701) 49
    195.219.67.201 (metric 180) from 216.218.252.157 (216.218.252.157)
      Origin IGP, metric 60, localpref 100, valid, internal
      Community: 6939:2000
  6453 UUNET/ALTERNET (701) 49
    64.86.84.153 (metric 757) from 216.218.252.145 (216.218.252.145)
      Origin IGP, metric 60, localpref 100, valid, internal
      Community: 6939:2000
  6453 UUNET/ALTERNET (701) 49
    66.198.97.17 (metric 764) from 216.218.252.146 (216.218.252.146)
      Origin IGP, metric 60, localpref 100, valid, internal
      Community: 6939:2000
  WCG (7911) UUNET/ALTERNET (701) 49
    64.200.86.153 (metric 100) from 216.66.23.99 (216.66.23.99)
      Origin IGP, metric 47, localpref 100, valid, internal, best
      Community: 6939:2000 7911:999 7911:7307
  WCG (7911) UUNET/ALTERNET (701) 49
    64.200.88.13 from 64.200.88.13 (64.200.95.239)
      Origin IGP, metric 48, localpref 100, valid, external
      Community: 6939:2000 7911:999 7911:7307
  WCG (7911) UUNET/ALTERNET (701) 49
    64.200.61.185 (metric 350) from 216.218.252.154 (216.218.252.154)
      Origin IGP, metric 60, localpref 100, valid, internal Community: 6939:2000
  WCG (7911) UUNET/ALTERNET (701) 49
    64.200.104.121 (metric 380) from 216.218.252.155 (216.218.252.155)
      Origin IGP, metric 60, localpref 100, valid, internal
      Community: 6939:2000
  WCG (7911) UUNET/ALTERNET (701) 49
    64.200.139.153 (metric 741) from 216.218.252.153 (216.218.252.153)
      Origin IGP, metric 60, localpref 100, valid, internal
      Community: 6939:2000 7911:999 7911:7303
```

Figure 2-2. Routing Table Entries for Paths to NIST's 129.6.0.0/16 Addresses

2.4 BGP   Standards

BGP is defined by a number of standards (for historical reasons called Request for Comments [RFC]) maintained by the Internet Engineering Task Force (IETF). BGP protocol version 4, the current BGP version, plus extensions to this protocol are defined in the following documents:

RFC 1771, *A Border Gateway Protocol 4 (BGP-4)* – this is the base document defining the BGP protocol. It is an Internet standard that is used by all BGP implementations, although it includes significant flexibility in implementation. (Note: RFC 4271 obsoletes RFC 1771).

RFC 1772, *Application of the Border Gateway Protocol in the Internet* – with its companion document, RFC 1771 (which is now RFC 4271), this publication defines how BGP is to be implemented in routers.

RFC 1930, *Guidelines for creation, selection, and registration of an Autonomous System (AS)* – this is a guideline explaining when an organization needs and should use an autonomous system. It is an informative document, rather than a standard.

RFC 1997, *BGP Communities Attribute* – establishes an optional path attribute called COMMUNITIES, designed to simplify the control and distribution of routing information by allowing routing decisions to be based on the identity of a group.

RFC 2270, *Using a Dedicated AS for Sites Homed to a Single Provider* – this is a guideline designed to resolve problems that arise when a site is homed to a single ISP. It is an informative document, rather than a standard.

RFC 2283, *Multiprotocol Extensions for BGP-4* – defines extensions to the BGP4 protocol to allow it to carry routing information for IPv6 and other network layer protocols. Because the extensions are upwards compatible, a BGP 4 implementation can interoperate with one that supports the extensions.

RFC 2385, *Protection of BGP Sessions via the TCP MD5 Signature Option* – defines a TCP extension to improve BGP security by specifying an option to include an MD5 signature in a TCP message. This procedure provides much stronger authentication of BGP messages.

RFC 2439, *BGP Route Flap Damping* – defines the route flap damping algorithm, which reduces the volume of routing traffic between BGP peers. Commercial routers normally implement this important BGP feature.

IETF, RFC 2918 – *Route Refresh Capability for BGP-4* – defines a BGP capability to allow dynamic exchange of route refresh information on request between BGP speakers.

RFC 2545, *Use of BGP-4 Multiprotocol Extensions for IPv6 Inter-Domain Routing* – specifies how BGP implementations should use the BGP attribute MP_REACH_NLRI and MP_UNREACH_NLRI, which are used to announce and withdraw reachability information.

RFC 4456, *BGP Route Reflection: An Alternative to Full-Mesh IBGP* – obsoletes RFC 2796, described above.

RFC 2827 (BCP 38), *Network Ingress Filtering: Defeating Denial of Service Attacks which Employ IP Source Address Spoofing* – this is a Best Current Practice document that provides practical methods to filter incoming traffic to prevent denial of service attacks that use forged IP addresses.

RFC 3065, *Autonomous System Confederations for BGP* – defines an extension to BGP that can be used to create a confederation of multiple autonomous systems. The confederation of systems appears as a single AS to BGP peers outside of the confederation. This protocol is designed to remove the "full mesh" requirement of BGP, to reduce administration and maintenance costs for large autonomous systems.

RFC 3562, "Key Management Considerations for the TCP MD5 Signature Option," – The security of the TCP MD5 Signature Option (RFC 2385) relies heavily on the quality of the keying material used to compute the MD5 signature. This RFC addresses the security requirements of that keying material.

RFC 3682, *Generalized TTL Security Mechanism (GTSM)* – This experimental protocol, often referred to as the "TTL hack", sets the TTL to 255 on outgoing packets. Since routers decrement the

TTL field by one when a packet is forwarded, adjacent peers should see incoming packets with a TTL of 255. To implement GTSM, routers are set to ignore packets with a TTL of less than 254 (to allow for some variations in router implementations).

RFC 3765, *NOPEER Community for Border Gateway Protocol (BGP) Route Scope Control* – explains the use of the NOPEER advisory transitive community attribute, which allows an origin AS to indicate that a route does not need to be advertised across bilateral peer connections.

RFC 3768, Virtual Router Redundancy Protocol – describes a protocol for establishment and maintenance of hot-standby routers that can provide continuity of BGP operations if a router is disabled.

RFC 4264, BGP Wedgies – BGP Wedgie refers to a stable but unintended (and generally undesirable) forwarding state. This condition can occur where states other than the intended forwarding state are equally stable and BGP converges to a stable state in a non-deterministic manner.

RFC 4271, A Border Gateway Protocol 4 (BGP-4) – provides a set of mechanisms for supporting Classless Inter-Domain Routing (CIDR). These mechanisms include support for advertising a set of destinations as an IP prefix, and eliminating the concept of network "class" within BGP. BGP-4 also introduces mechanisms that allow aggregation of routes, including aggregation of AS paths. (RFC 4271 obsoletes RFC 1771).

RFC 4272, BGP Security Vulnerabilities Analysis – discusses the security issues with BGP routing data dissemination and vulnerabilities of BGP, based on the BGP specification [RFC4271].

RFC 4276, BGP-4 Implementation Report – documents BGP implementation details from Alcatel, Cisco, Laurel, and NextHop and summarizes BGP implementations of Avici, Data Connection, and Nokia. Useful in understanding how options of the BGP-4 standard (RFC 4271) are handled by different implementers.

RFC 4277, Experience with the BGP-4 Protocol – provides an overview of BGP and reports practical considerations for various aspects of BGP operation such as route flap damping, BGP over IPsec, MD5 signatures, and others.

RFC 4301, Security Architecture for the Internet Protocol – specifies the base architecture for IPsec-compliant systems; describes how to provide a set of security services for traffic at the IP layer in both the IPv4 and IPv6 environments; describes the security services offered by the IPsec protocols, and how these services can be employed in the IP environment. (Obsoletes RFC 2401)

RFC 4302 through 4309 – RFCs supplementary to RFC 4301; describe the Authentication Header (AH) protocol [RFC 4302] and Encapsulating Security Payload (ESP) protocol [RFC 4303]; describe cryptographic algorithms for integrity and encryption -- RFC 4305 defines the mandatory, default cryptographic algorithms for use with AH and ESP, and RFC 4307 defines the mandatory cryptographic algorithms for use with the Internet Key Exchange (IKEv2) protocol; describe automatic key management (AKM) procedures -- RFC 4306 describes AKM for the IKEv2 protocol.

RFC 4456, *BGP Route Reflection: An Alternative to Full-Mesh IBGP* – defines an experimental protocol that is designed to alleviate scaling problems that derive from the need to distribute external routing information to all routers within an AS.

RFC 4778, Operational Security Current Practices in Internet Service Provider Environments – documents currently deployed security mechanisms for layer 2 and layer 3 network infrastructure devices. Although it primarily focused on IPv4, many of the same practices can (and should) apply to IPv6 networks as well.

RIPE-229, *RIPE Routing-WG Recommendations for Coordinated Route-flap Damping Parameters* – specifies route flap damping configuration for ISPs, to reduce the risk of denial of service attacks that seek to trigger large scale flap damping. RIPE-229 prevents critical routes (such as root DNS servers) from being damped, and uses a weighting scheme to slow down damping of other important routes. (RIPE-229 has been obsoleted by RIPE-378.)

RIPE-378, *Recommendations on Route-flap Damping*, RIPE Routing Working Group (obsoletes RIPE-229, RIPE-210, RIPE-178), 11 May 2006. Updates recommendations on route flap damping based on current research that indicates RFD can contribute to several security problems. RIPE-378 recommends against using RFD, although in certain cases it may be appropriate.

These RFCs and drafts can be found at the IETF Web site at http://www.ietf.org/.

3. BGP Risks, Threats, and Mitigation Techniques

Like many other protocols, BGP was designed long before security became a serious issue for the Internet. In particular, BGP does not have a built-in authentication mechanism to ensure that a message is really from the AS that is shown as the source in messages. As a result, BGP retains a number of vulnerabilities, despite extensions designed to shore up its security. Fortunately, many of the methods developed over the years to improve BGP's dependability also contribute to security against outside attackers. For example, route flap damping and ingress/egress filtering policies have helped to make BGP both more stable and more secure. In addition, the more precise addressing allowed by classless interdomain routing (CIDR) makes it possible to refine the handling of prefixes in BGP, providing a further level of protection from accidental or malicious changes to routing tables. Insider attacks, either malicious or accidental, are a second concern. Some of the countermeasures discussed in this document help resist both external and internal attacks, but threats from insiders require extra measures of access control enforced within an organization.

One of the primary risks from attacks on BGP is loss of connectivity between critical portions of the Internet; that is, email, e-commerce, and Web accesses would not function. Because of the volume of commercial transactions conducted over the Internet, plus increasing use of the Internet for voice communications (voice over IP [VOIP]), such an outage could have a significant impact on the economy, and possibly interrupt critical functions such as emergency services communications. The outage could be either widespread, affecting large portions of the Internet, or a targeted denial of service attack against a particular organization's network.

A second security concern for BGP is confidentiality, particularly the confidentiality risks arising from misrouting of packets. Internet communication is not secure unless special measures are taken, such as encryption, and most users do not encrypt email or other traffic. An eavesdropper could mount an attack by changing routing tables to redirect traffic through nodes that can be monitored. The attacker could thus monitor the contents or source and destination of the redirected traffic, or modify it maliciously.

This section explores significant risks to BGP operation and outlines countermeasures that can minimize these risks. Countermeasures are rated for effectiveness and cost as Low (L), Medium (M), or High (H). These ratings are necessarily subjective and intended as an approximate guide only. Actual cost and effectiveness will vary with the installation. Comprehensive BGP security solutions have not yet emerged and current "best common practices" are somewhat overlapping, confusing in scope and applicability, and often neglect cost/benefit tradeoffs. The following sections provide more specific configuration details and checklists of security-related features to assist in procurement of BGP equipment. For more information on the RFC standards cited in this section, see Section 2.4.

3.1 Generic   Attacks

As with other networked devices, routers are subject to denial of service, unauthorized access, eavesdropping, packet manipulation, session hijacking, and other attacks. Attacks on BGP, detailed in the next section, are extensions or specializations of these.

Denial of service, potentially the greatest risk to BGP, occurs when a router is flooded with more packets than it can handle. The attack often involves a large number of compromised hosts (a distributed denial of service attack). A denial of service attack could come about through a number of ways, including:

— Starvation – a node receives fewer packets than it should because traffic is sent to nodes that cannot deliver it

- Blackhole – traffic is sent to routers that drop some or all of the packets

- Delay – traffic is forwarded through sub-optimal paths

- Looping – packets enter a looping path, so that the traffic is never delivered

- Network partition – a portion of the network appears to be partitioned from the rest of the network because of faulty routing information

- Churn – rapid changes in packet forwarding disrupt packet delivery, possibly affecting congestion control

- Instability – convergence to a single global forwarding state does not occur

- Network overload – the network begins carrying an excessive number of BGP messages, overloading the router control processors and reducing the bandwidth available for data traffic

- Router resource exhaustion – router resources (storage or processing cycles) are exhausted by excess BGP messages.

Inducing a "BGP Wedgie" can be a potential attack vector. BGP wedgie refers to a stable but unintended (and generally undesirable) forwarding state (see RFC 4264). This condition can occur where states other than the intended forwarding state are equally stable and BGP converges to a stable state in a non-deterministic manner. RFC 4264 describes the potential security exploitation of BGP wedgies as follows. A common theme of BGP wedgies is that starting from an intended or desired forwarding state, the loss and subsequent restoration of an eBGP peering connection can flip the network's forwarding configuration into an unintended and potentially undesired state. Significant administrative effort – based on BGP state and configuration knowledge that may not be locally available – may be required to shift the BGP forwarding configuration back to the intended or desired forwarding state. If a hostile third party can deliberately cause the BGP session to reset, thereby producing the initial conditions that lead to an unintended forwarding state, the network impacts of the resulting unintended or undesired forwarding state may be long-lived, far outliving the temporary interruption of connectivity that triggered the condition. If these impacts of BGP wedgie, including potential issues of increased cost, reduction of available bandwidth, increases in overall latency or degradation of service reliability, are significant, then disrupting a BGP session could represent an attractive attack vector to a hostile party.

Unauthorized access can occur when default passwords and community strings (which control access to Simple Network Management Protocol [SNMP] services) are not changed, or passwords are guessed. Social engineering or exploitation of software flaws may also lead to unauthorized access.

Eavesdropping of BGP packets may occur anywhere on the path between routers, since BGP messages are not encrypted, or BGP may be exploited to allow eavesdropping on application data packets.

Packet manipulation methods include inserting false IP addresses to gain access or inject false data into routing tables, or rerouting packets for purposes of blackholing, eavesdropping, or traffic analysis.

Session hijacking occurs when an intruder uses falsified packets to take over or continue an authorized session.

3.2 Potential Attacks on BGP

While not an exhaustive list, the attacks discussed in this section are the most common that are likely to be a concern for BGP. Some, such as spoofing and session hijacking, are variants on common TCP/IP protocol attacks, while those that involve route manipulation are more specific to BGP and related routing protocols. Since BGP runs on TCP/IP, any TCP/IP attack can be applied to BGP. As noted, denial of service and eavesdropping are among the primary risks from BGP attacks, but a number of subsidiary issues are involved, as detailed in an IETF RFC 4272, *BGP Security Vulnerabilities Analysis* [44] (terms explained below are often seen in discussions of BGP vulnerabilities).

3.2.1 Peer Spoofing and TCP Resets

Spoofing attacks are a concern for all network protocols. *Spoofing* refers to transmission of packets that are modified to make them appear as if they originate from somewhere other than their true source. With ordinary TCP connections under IPv4, it is easy to disguise the source address of an IP connection. When applied to BGP, this means that the spoofed source must be that of one of the BGP speaker's peer routers. The goal of the spoofing attack may be to insert false information into a BGP peer's routing tables. Peer IP addresses can often be found using the ICMP *traceroute* function, so BGP implementations should include countermeasures against this attack.

A special case of peer spoofing, called a *reset attack,* involves inserting TCP RESET messages into an ongoing session between two BGP peers [5][66]. BGP is carried over TCP (the same protocol used for common Internet communications such as Web browsing). By monitoring communication between two BGP peers, an attacker may gain enough information to send a forged reset message to one of the routers (see Figure 3-1).

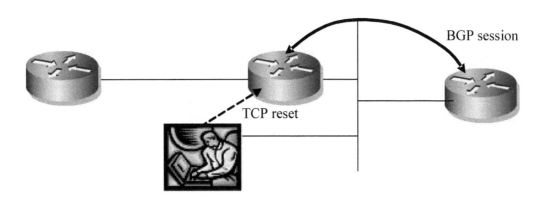

Figure 3-1. TCP Reset Attack

When a reset is received, the target router drops the BGP session and both peers withdraw routes previously learned from each other, thus disrupting network connectivity until recovery, which may take several minutes to hours, depending on the number of BGP peers affected. This attack is more difficult to accomplish than spoofing the source of a new session, because in addition to the source IP address, the source port of the session must be known, and the sequence number must fit into the ongoing connection. While possible, an attack such as this that relies on knowing sequence numbers is more difficult than other attacks, and countermeasures are relatively good at defeating it [39][31][5][8].

Table 3-1. Peer Spoofing Countermeasures

Method	Reference or RFC	Strength	Cost	Notes
Strong sequence number randomization	CERT Advisory CA-2001-09 [5]	M	L	Varies with the underlying operating system See Section 4.3
TTL Hack	RFC 3682	M	L	Simple configuration option; not effective against machines one hop away See Section 4.4
MD5 Signature option	RFC 2385	H	M	Widely available option; may be significant administrative cost See Section 4.5

3.2.2 TCP Resets Using ICMP

The Internet Control Message Protocol (ICMP) can also be used to produce session resets [53]. This attack can be substantially easier than the session reset described in Section 3.2.1, because current IETF specifications do not require checking sequence numbers of received ICMP messages. These attacks require knowledge of the victim's IP address and port number, but the nature of BGP requires that they be known. As a result, it is easy for attackers to send spoofed ICMP hard or soft error messages, which cause TCP session reset (hard errors) or signal performance/throughput degradation (soft errors). TCP resets cause loss of BGP peering sessions, forcing a need to rebuild routing tables and possibly causing route flapping. The primary countermeasure is checking that the TCP sequence number is within the range of packets sent but not yet acknowledged, i.e., $SND.UNA \leq SEG.SEQ < SND.NXT$. This and other aspects of countermeasures to ICMP-based TCP reset attacks are discussed in [18][53].

Table 3-2. TCP Reset Countermeasures

Method	Reference or RFC	Strength	Cost	Notes
TCP sequence number checking	[18][53]	M	L	Varies with the underlying operating System. Included on Linux, FreeBSD, OpenBSD.
TTL Hack	RFC 3682	M	L	Simple configuration option; not effective against machines one hop away See Section 4.4
Router access control	[18]	H M		Block packets of ICMP Type 3 codes 2, 3, and 4 See also NISCC Vulnerability Advisory ICMP – 532967 [53]
IPsec authentication	[45]	H	M	Widely available; may be significant administrative cost See Section 4.6.

3.2.3 Session   Hijacking

Like the TCP reset attack, session hijacking involves intrusion into an ongoing BGP session, i.e., the attacker successfully masquerades as one of the peers in a BGP session, and requires the same information needed to accomplish the reset attack. The difference is that a session hijacking attack may be designed to achieve more than simply bringing down a session between BGP peers. For example, the objective may be to change routes used by the peer, in order to facilitate eavesdropping, blackholing, or traffic analysis.

Table 3-3. Session Hijacking Countermeasures

Method	Reference or RFC	Strength	Cost	Notes
Strong sequence number randomization	CERT Advisory CA-2001-09 [5]	M	L	Varies with the underlying operating system See Section 4.3
TTL Hack	RFC 3682	M	L	Simple configuration option; not effective against machines one hop away
MD5 Signature option	RFC 2385	H	M	Widely available option; may be significant administrative cost See Section 4.5
IPsec	RFC 4301, plus many related RFCs (RFCs 4302-4309)	H	H	See Section 4.6

3.2.4 Route Flapping

Route flapping refers to repetitive changes to the BGP routing table, often several times a minute. A "route flap" occurs when a route is withdrawn and then re-advertised. High-rate route flapping can cause a serious problem for routers, because every flap causes route changes or withdrawals that propagate through the network of ASes. If route flaps happen fast enough – e.g., 30 to 50 times per second – the router becomes overloaded, eventually preventing convergence on valid routes. The potential impact for Internet users is a slowdown in message delivery, and in some cases packets may not be received at all. In other words, route flapping can result in a denial of service, either accidental or from an intentional attack [32][61].

Route flap damping is a method of reducing route flaps by implementing an algorithm that ignores the router sending flapping updates for a configurable period of time [32]. Each time a flapping event occurs, peer routers add a penalty value to a total for the flapping router. The penalty decays exponentially over time, according to the equation $P(t') = P(t)2^{-\lambda(t'-t)}$, where $P(t)$ is the penalty at time t, t' is a future time ($t' > t$), and λ is a configurable parameter ($1/\lambda$ = half-time of the decay). If route flaps persist often enough, the total exceeds a configurable cutoff threshold (see Figure 3-2). At this point, routes learned from the flapping router are withdrawn, and peers recompute their route table entries and updates are propagated across the network. As time passes, the penalty value decays gradually; if no further flaps are seen, it will reach a reuse threshold, at which time the peer will resume accepting routes from the previously flapping router.

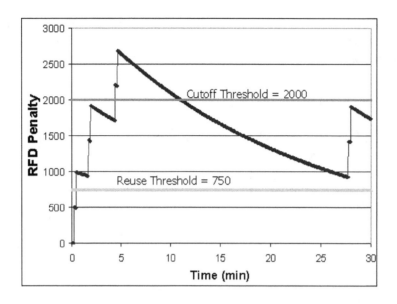

Figure 3-2. Penalty Accumulation in Route Flap Damping

While this mechanism helps to reduce instability caused by spontaneous faults in the network, it can be misused by an attacker. If a router can be disabled, even temporarily, its BGP sessions will be disrupted and peer routers will begin routing around it, assuming it is down. This process can trigger changes throughout the network, leading to increased load, and possibly causing traffic to slow down as routing changes result in less optimal forwarding. By this means, a compromised router that is disabled repeatedly can cause disruption that might extend beyond what would occur if the router were simply shut down. (If the router were permanently disabled, other routers would quickly find paths around it.) Repeated BGP peering session attacks (e.g., via TCP resets or spoofed ICMP error messages) can also be used to cause route flapping and withdrawal of routes to parts of the network. The RFD mechanism is exploited in this attack mode to amplify the route outages drastically [61].

Table 3-4. Route Flap Countermeasures

Method	Reference or RFC	Strength	Cost	Notes
Graceful Restart	[58]	M	M	Both performance and security benefits; must be supported by both peers; effective up to very high attack rates [61] See Section 5.1
BGP Route Flap Damping w/ recommended parameters and RIPE Routing-WG Recommendations for Coordinated Route-Flap Damping Parameters	RFC 2439 RIPE-229	M	L	RFD can mitigate effects of route flapping in certain limited scenarios, but one should heed cautions about potential RFD problems and abuses. See Section5.1, RIPE-378 [59], and [61]. RIPE-229 specifies a "graded damping" approach; used in association with RFC 2439

Because of the potential problems described above, and the fact that faster processors in routers have obviated some of the original need for RFD, network administrators should be cautious about enabling RFD. Some current guidance (see in particular RIPE-378 [59]) recommends against using RFD, but in selected situations it may be useful. For example, RFD may help in isolating parts of the network where attacks are in progress, limiting the spread of damage. BGP administrators should weigh the potential risks carefully before enabling RFD. Recommendations may change as additional research is completed.

3.2.5 Route   Deaggregation

Route deaggregation occurs when more specific (i.e., longer prefix) routes are advertised by BGP peers. For example, if prefixes 129.0.0.0/8 and 129.0.0.0/16 are both advertised, BGP algorithms will select the second (for any addresses within 129.0.0.0/16) because it is more specific. In some cases this is normal and appropriate operation as a result of configuration changes, but it can occur as a result of error or malicious activity. The primary impact of such an event is a degradation of service that, in some cases, can be widespread. In 1997, a configuration error at one AS caused it to deaggregate routes, i.e., announce more specific routes (/24 paths) for most of the Internet. In other words, it was effectively announcing that it had optimal paths to all destinations. Because BGP gives preference to the most specific routes, a huge number of updates with thousands of new routes spread quickly, causing router crashes and shutting down major ISPs for two hours.

Route deaggregation could also occur as a result of malicious activity. If a BGP peer receives a prefix that is more specific (for a particular address block) than those in its routing table, it will update the table with the more specific prefix, and propagate the new route to other peers. A situation similar to the 1997 route deaggregation failure mentioned above could be triggered if an AS were compromised and more specific routes sent out to its peers. Alternatively, BGP updates could be forged to appear to come from a valid AS.

Avoiding compromise of a router is a basic requirement to prevent attackers from causing a malicious route deaggregation. Thus, ordinary steps required to secure an individual router are an essential first step (see Section 4.8). A secondary requirement is to prevent the spread of deaggregated prefixes through the Internet.

One available approach is to establish a maximum prefix limit [63]. A limit can be pre-set that causes the router to disable or terminate a session and issue warning messages when a neighbor sends in excess of a preset number of prefixes. Deaggregation of routes would trigger the prefix limiting feature, and the session with that peer would be disabled until it was manually restored, giving operators an opportunity to detect the problem and prevent it from spreading through the Internet. As with most security features, however, there is a tradeoff between defenses for types of possible attacks. Using prefix limiting could allow a denial of service attack if a stream of deaggregated prefix messages can be forged to come from the victim router. Its peers would then disable connections to the victim router. However, the disruption would be temporary, and operators would be able to intervene to restore connections.

Table 3-5. Route Deaggregation Countermeasures

Method	Ref. or RFC	Strength	Cost	Notes
Max Prefix-Limit feature	[63]	M	L	Configuration option on some routers
Route filtering	[35]	M	M	See Section 4.2
Secure router administration		M	L	See Section 4.8

3.2.6 Malicious Route Injection

BGP exists to spread routing information across the Internet. Routers tell each other what prefixes they can reach and provide data on how efficiently they can reach addresses within these prefixes. In a benign, cooperative environment this works well, but a malicious party could begin sending out updates with incorrect routing information. For example, NIST's address space is 129.6.0.0/16 (see Section 2.2). Suppose that NIST announces 129.6.0.0/16 through BGP. An attacker who announces a more specific route, such as a /24 address in NIST's IP address space, would be able to divert packets that should be sent to NIST. This would occur because other routers would view the /24 as a more direct route (see Section 2.2) to some of the addresses within NIST, so packets would be routed to the attacker's machine, which could observe and record the packets' data and address information. NIST would have no control over the routes announced by the attacker, other than contacting the attacker's service provider to request a correction, and it would be difficult to prove whether the mis-routing was malicious or accidental. In fact, NIST may not even see the attacker's route announcement, since it would be discarded locally by BGP to prevent route loops. Note that a similar risk occurs when an attacker gains control of a BGP router and forces it to announce a less specific route, such as a /15. In this case, traffic would flow to neighboring BGP routers that are announcing more specific (/16 or longer) paths, possibly overloading these routers.

Consequences could include eavesdropping – causing other nodes to route information through the attacker's node; and denial of service – traffic that otherwise would be forwarded efficiently is sent via slower routes or disappears entirely. Malicious route injection of this kind is possible because standard BGP has no authentication to guarantee the identity of BGP peers, and no authorization mechanism to ensure that a BGP peer has the authority to update routes to particular prefixes. Route filtering and MD5 authentication primarily address the first of these issues.

A variety of research projects have been initiated to address these problems. Most solutions are based either on cryptographic techniques that can guarantee the authenticity of announcements [2], or on data-driven approaches that track BGP traffic for a period of time so that faulty or fraudulent announcements can be detected by comparing with historical data [47]. These methods are often difficult to apply on a large scale, so they have not seen significant adoption. Until one or more of these proposed solutions are adopted widely, basic mechanisms described in this document can add to the security of BGP.

Table 3-6. Malicious Route Injection Countermeasures

Method	Reference or RFC	Strength	Cost	Notes
Route filtering	[34]	M M		Configuration option See Section 4.2
MD5 Signature option	RFC 2385	H	M	Widely available option; may be significant administrative cost See Section 4.5

3.2.7 Unallocated Route Injection

A particular variety of malicious route injection involves the transmission of routes to unallocated prefixes. These prefixes specify sets of IP addresses that have not been assigned yet, i.e., no one should be using these addresses, so no traffic should be routed to them. Therefore, any route information for these prefixes is clearly faulty or malicious, and should be dropped.

Table 3-7. Unallocated Route Injection Countermeasures

Method	Reference or RFC	Strength	Cost	Notes
Drop unallocated prefixes	[22][62] M M			Prefix list must be continually updated See Section 4.2.2
Route filtering	[35]	M	M	See Section 4.2
MD5 Signature option	RFC 2385	H	M	Widely available option; may be significant administrative cost See Section 4.5

Additional notes: Drop unallocated ("bogon") prefixes – Care must be taken to ensure that valid prefixes are not denied. As the Internet grows, prefixes are allocated to new nodes, so unallocated route lists become obsolete quickly. In addition, some allocated prefixes may be returned, thus becoming unallocated. Reserved address blocks may also change. A list of assigned IPv4 blocks is maintained by the Internet Assigned Number Authority (IANA) [22]. A list of bogon prefixes is maintained by Team-Cymru [62]. This list should be consulted regularly as part of the BGP administrative process. See the Secure BGP Template (Section 4.1) for more information on keeping route lists up to date.

3.2.8 Denial of Service via Resource Exhaustion

Like all computers, routers have a finite amount of storage and processing cycles available. One of the most common attacks of this type is known as a "SYN flood", in which a large number of TCP/IP communication sessions are started using the SYN (synchronization) packet, without follow-up by the appropriate next packet type. This causes the receiving host to reserve storage space for the session. With enough SYN packets, space is eventually exhausted on the host. Since BGP is implemented on TCP/IP, BGP processing can be affected by this attack. In addition to storage needed by the underlying TCP/IP processing, routers use a large amount of storage for path prefixes. These resources can be exhausted if updates are received too rapidly or if there are too many path prefixes to store due to malicious prefix announcements. A variety of countermeasures are available for these attacks. An Internet Draft that describes SYN flood mitigation methods is available at the IETF web site (see [15]).

Table 3-8. Resource Exhaustion Countermeasures

Method	Reference or RFC	Strength	Cost	Notes
Rate limit syn processing	[12][15]	M	L	May be a configurable option on some routers
Increase queue length		L	L	May be a configurable option on some routers
Route filtering		L	M	See Section 4.2
TTL Hack	RFC 3682	M	L	Simple configuration option; helps prevent DoS floods on port 179 See Section 4.4; not effective against machines one hop away

3.2.9 Link Cutting Attack

An inherent vulnerability in routing protocols is their potential for manipulation by cutting links in the network [3]. By removing links, either through denial of service or physical attacks, an attacker can divert traffic to allow for eavesdropping, blackholing, or traffic analysis. Because routing protocols are designed to find paths around broken links, these attacks are particularly hard to defend against.

Table 3-9. Link Cutting Attack Countermeasures

Method	Reference or RFC	Strength	Cost	Notes
Encryption	IPsec	H	H	Not fully effective against traffic analysis; not effective against blackholing See Section 4.6
Intrusion detection systems	[3]	M	H	Experimental for this attack; not widely used
Redundant backup paths to make it difficult to divert traffic to nodes not under your control	M		H	Very expensive to maintain; not available to most organizations See Section 4.8

In a link-cutting attack, the attacker owns, or has compromised, one or more ASes. With knowledge of routes in the network, the attacker can determine what links need to be cut to force traffic through the compromised node. In effect, the attacker wants to create a situation where the compromised node is the only path from one point in the network to others, allowing the observation of packets forced through this node.

4. Details   of Countermeasures and Security Mechanisms

As originally designed, BGP has no built-in security functionality. Several alternative BGP protocols have been proposed, but none widely implemented. Alternatively, one practical approach today to securing BGP is to adopt countermeasures listed in the previous section. This section describes these options in more detail, and provides references for additional information.

4.1   The Secure BGP Template

The Secure BGP Template is a useful collection of BGP configuration settings for Cisco routers, made available by Team-Cymru [63]. It is widely used and should be considered during the procurement and configuration of BGP. This section provides a non-vendor specific discussion of the secure BGP template; following sections cover many of the topics noted here, and other security mechanisms, in greater depth.

Do not require synchronization with IBGP. BGP synchronization refers to a requirement that BGP wait until the IGP propagates a newly learned route within the AS before advertising the route to external peers. This feature is generally deprecated and not supported by all vendors as Internet routing tables are now extremely large and can consume excessive resources, in addition to placing unnecessary stress on the IGP as a result of the need to carry extra routes.

Turn off fast external failover to avoid major route changes due to transient failures of peers to send keepalives. The "fast external failover" feature was designed to allow rapid failover to an alternate system when a link goes down. Without this feature, failover would not occur until BGP keepalive timers would permit recognition that the line had failed. It is not uncommon for lines to drop BGP sessions and then return, referred to as route flapping (see Section 3.2.4). Frequent flapping can trigger flap damping in upstream peers. Due to fast external failovers, flap damping would occur at upstream routers, which in turn results in prolonged peer-prefix unreachability and system instability. So turning off fast external failover normally represents a positive tradeoff in today's Internet.

Record peer changes. Logging whenever a peer enters or leaves Established state provides useful records for debugging or audit trails for investigating possible security problems.

Announce netblocks with a view towards lower CPU utilization as well as reduced eBGP-update dynamics. Avoid unnecessary dynamic coupling of IGP and eBGP to prevent propagation of instability from IGP to eBGP (and vice versa).

Use soft reconfiguration. Normally a change in policy requires BGP sessions to be cleared before the new policy can be initiated, resulting in a need to rebuild sessions with consequent impact on routing performance. Thus, spoofed policy changes could be used for a denial of service attack, even if the policy changes themselves do not violate AS rules. Soft reconfiguration allows new policies to be initiated without resetting sessions. It is done on a per-peer basis, and can be set up for either or both inbound and outbound [6][55] (for updates from and to neighbors, respectively).

A recent improvement to soft reconfiguration is Route Refresh (RFC 2918 [36]). The route refresh capability allows dynamic exchange of route refresh requests between BGP peers, to obtain a re-advertisement of Adj-RIB-Out. This capability avoids the need to store unmodified copies of the routes learned from peers at all times.

Use authentication. Authentication is one of the strongest mechanisms for preventing malicious activity. Use IPsec or MD5, if available (see Section 4.5 and Section 4.6).

Disable BGP version negotiation to provide faster startup. Since peers change infrequently, BGP versions for known peers can be established statically rather than renegotiated each time BGP restarts.

Block inbound announcements of bogon prefixes. Since these prefixes do not represent valid routes, they should not be announced or propagated (see Section 4.2.2).

Announce only preconfigured list of networks.

Use max prefix limits to avoid filling router tables. Routers should be configured to disable or terminate a session and issue warning messages to administrators when a neighbor sends in excess of a preset number of prefixes.

Use loopback interface for IBGP announcements.

Do not auto summarize announcements. Auto summarization causes the router to summarize network paths according to traditional Class A, B, C, and D boundaries. This behavior can be problematic if, for example, the AS does not own the complete classed network that is summarized.

Allow peers to connect to port 179 only. The standard port for receiving BGP session OPENs is port 179, so attempts by peers to reach other ports are likely to indicate faulty configuration or potential malicious activity.

Set announce prefix list to allow announcing only designated netblocks. This option will prevent the router from inadvertently providing transit to networks not listed by the AS (see Section 4.2).

Filter all bogon prefixes. These prefixes (see Section 4.2.2) are invalid, so they should not appear in routes. Filtering them reduces load and helps reduce the ability of attackers to use forged addresses in denial of service or other attacks.

Do not allow over-specific prefixes (see Section 4.2.3 for discussion of which prefixes should be designated "over-specific"). Requiring routers to maintain large numbers of very specific prefixes can place excessive load on system resources.

4.2 Prefix   Filtering

Prefix filtering is the most basic mechanism for protecting BGP routers from accidental or malicious disruption. Filtering of both incoming prefixes *(ingress filtering)*, and outgoing prefixes (*egress filtering*) is needed. Router filters are specified using syntax similar to that for firewalls. One option is to list ranges of IP prefixes that are to be denied, then permit all others. Alternatively, ranges of permitted prefixes can be specified, and the rest denied. This option will normally provide greater security. The choice of which approach to use depends on practical considerations determined by system administrators.

Normally, BGP peers should have matching prefix filters, i.e., the egress filters of an AS should be matched by the ingress filters of peers with which it communicates. For example, if AS 100 filters its outgoing prefixes to only those in set P, and AS 200 is a BGP peer, then AS 200 establishes ingress filters to ensure that the prefixes it accepts from AS 100 are only those in set P. This approach helps to reduce the risk from attackers that seek to inject false routes by pretending to send updates from AS 100 to its peers. Attackers can of course still send faulty routes to the prefixes in set P, but filtering helps to limit the damage to these routes and no further.

4.2.1 Special Use Addresses

Among the prefixes that should never be routed are the special use prefixes, such as those used for internal networks behind a network address translation router (e.g., 192.168.0.0/16). An IETF draft, draft-manning-dsua-08.txt, lists these and explains their use [50] Prefixes in this draft have been registered with the Internet Assigned Numbers Authority (IANA) as reserved for special purposes. Currently they are:

0.0.0.0/8 and 0.0.0.0/32 – broadcast and default addresses

127.0.0.0/8 – loopback address used in testing IP protocol software, and sometimes used to implement local proxy servers such as those for spam filters

192.0.2.0/24 – reserved for testing

10.0.0.0/8 – used in private networks, such as those behind a network address translation (NAT) router (see RFC 1918)

172.16.0.0/12 – used in private networks, such as those behind a NAT router (see RFC 1918)

192.168.0.0/16 – used in private networks, such as those behind a NAT router (see RFC 1918)

169.254.0.0/16 – used for auto-configuration when a Dynamic Host Configuration Protocol (DHCP) server is not found

192.88.99.0/24 – RFC 3068 Anycast prefix

all class D space – multicast addresses; four highest order bits are set to 1110

all class E space – unspecified reserved; four highest order bits are set to 1111.

Sample rules to filter these addresses given in the draft [50] are shown below in the following format:
access-list # | permit or deny | ip or icmp | source | source mask | destination | destination mask
(For masks x.x.x.x, x = 0 → apply bits, x ≠ 0 → ignore bits; keyword "any" designates either a source or destination. Thus the second line denies any packet whose source address contains 127 in the first octet and destination contains 255 in the first octet.)

access-list 100 deny	ip	host	0.0.0.0		any	
access-list 100 deny	ip	127.0.0.0	0.255.255.255	255.0.0.0	0.255.255.255	
access-list 100 deny	ip	192.0.2.0	0.0.0.255	255.255.255.0	0.0.0.255	
access-list 100 deny	ip	10.0.0.0	0.255.255.255	255.0.0.0	0.255.255.255	
access-list 100 deny	ip	172.16.0.0	0.15.255.255	255.240.0.0	0.15.255.255	
access-list 100 deny	ip	192.168.0.0	0.0.255.255	255.255.0.0	0.0.255.255	
access-list 100 deny	ip	169.254.0.0	0.0.255.255	255.255.0.0	0.0.255.255	
access-list 100 deny	ip	240.0.0.0	15.255.255.255	any		
access-list 100 permit ip		any			any	

Rule syntax will of course vary with the router vendor and system administrator's choices regarding deny/permit placement.

4.2.2 "Bogon" Addresses

The term "bogon" (hacker slang derived from "bogus") refers to an IP address that is reserved but not yet allocated by IANA or some other Internet registry. Addresses that have not been allocated to legitimate users should never be routed, and packets that appear to come from these addresses are most likely forged. However, as the Internet grows, new addresses are continually allocated, so bogon address filters must be updated constantly. Failing to do so can result in segments of the network becoming unreachable. In 2004, some sites in New Zealand were blocked because they used addresses in the range 222.x.x.x. Many ISPs treated these addresses as unassigned and therefore invalid because they had failed to properly update their bogon filtering list with recently allocated IP addresses from Asia Pacific Network Information Centre (APNIC), the authorized registry for the New Zealand region.

Filtering bogon addresses can have a significant impact on security. One study found that bogon addresses were used as the source IP addresses for more than 60% of the packets that either violated access control rules or triggered intrusion detection. Filtering them out thus has a dual impact on security: eliminating packets that are likely to be malicious, and reducing the load on intrusion detection systems.

There are two approaches to mitigating the propagation and use of bogon addresses in BGP routing: route filtering and packet discarding. Because addresses are continually allocated as new nodes are added to the Internet, it is recommended that automated processes be used to maintain the lists of bogon addresses to filter or discard. The following sections describe sources of such information.

4.2.2.1 Bogon Address Updating

Following are some sources of current bogon address information.

Web-based bogon list

– List information: http://www.cymru.com/Documents/bogon-list.html

– Unaggregated (/8 addresses) list: http://www.cymru.com/Documents/bogon-bn-nonagg.txt

– Aggregated (including /7 addresses) list: http://www.cymru.com/Documents/bogon-bn-agg.txt

Bogon-announce list

– Subscribe to e-mail updates: https://puck.nether.net/mailman/listinfo/bogon-announce

– Archives: https://puck.nether.net/pipermail/bogon-announce/

4.2.2.2 BGP Bogon Route Server

BGP routers can obtain bogon filtering lists by peering with a bogon route-server, using a multihop session to a server that announces unaggregated bogon prefixes. The BGP community 65333:888 is included to identify the bogon information. Information on the bogon route server project is available at http://www.cymru.com/BGP/bogon-rs.html. This site maintains information on configuring popular routers to use the bogon route server. Note that this is an experimental, volunteer-run project, and its accuracy and continuation cannot be guaranteed. Other reliable sources may be needed.

4.2.3 IPv4 Filtering Guidelines

Filtering packets sent to and from BGP routers is an important component of security administration for BGP. Route updates can be filtered on the basis of route, path, or community attributes, and filters can be designed to deny specified prefixes and pass others, or pass specified prefixes and deny others. The method used can be decided by the system administrator based on configuration and policy requirements.

This section discusses generally accepted practices published in the NISCC BGP Filtering Guidelines [52] and other publications, and explains the reasoning behind these practices. Many of the practices included below are discussed in more detail elsewhere in this document.

1. Deny special prefixes assigned and reserved for future use – Reserved prefixes are set aside and not used for routing. For example, 192.168.0.0/16 is for local network use, so an external BGP peer should never have this IP address. (See Section 4.2.1.)

2. Deny unallocated (grey/bogon) space – Unallocated addresses have not been assigned to anyone and should therefore not be active. A BGP peer with an unallocated address is an anomaly, suggesting either a configuration error or malicious activity. (See Section 4.2.2.)

3. Deny over-specific prefix lengths – BGP reduces the volume of update messages by consolidating prefixes. Over-specific prefixes cause a large increase in the number of messages exchanged between peers. Recommendations vary as to what prefixes should be considered "over-specific", but a reasonable criterion could be those with prefix addresses in the range of /25 – /30.

4. Aggregate routes where possible – Routes are aggregated by using a shorter prefix to combine more than one address. For example, 36.0.0.0/7 can be used instead of 36.0.0.0/8 and 37.0.0.0/8 because the high order seven bits of binary 36 (0010 0100) are the same as the high order seven bits for binary 37 (0010 0101). Aggregating addresses saves space in routing tables and reduces the number of BGP messages that must be exchanged.

5. Deny exchange point prefixes (i.e., prefixes for links connecting ASes via an exchange point). These prefixes include the peering mesh (nodes connected directly to the AS) prefixes. ASes that are connected via an exchange point should not introduce the LAN address block of the exchange point in their IGP or eBGP. In addition, not announcing exchange point prefixes will make it more difficult for an attacker to send spoofed packets between distant points (i.e., directed towards an exchange point or across it). For more details see [65][63].

6. Deny routes to internal IP spaces – Internal IP addresses, such as those behind a NAT, should never be seen coming from an external peer, and should therefore be rejected. (See Section 4.2.1.)

4.2.4 Access Control Lists

Even older routers normally support some form of access control lists, which can be used to limit access to the router to only authorized systems. A basic set of access control rules will include the following, with the routers within an AS fully specified (/32 addresses):

1. Permit TCP connections from specified IBGP routers (any port) to specified EBGP routers (BGP port 179).

2. Permit TCP connections from specified IBGP routers (BGP port 179) to specified EBGP routers (any port).

3. Permit TCP connections from specified EBGP routers (any port) to specified EBGP routers (BGP port 179).

4. Permit TCP connections from specified EBGP routers (BGP port 179) to specified EBGP routers (any port).

5. Permit TCP connections from specified IBGP routers (any port) to specified IBGP routers (BGP port 179).

6. Permit TCP connections from specified IBGP routers (BGP port 179) to specified IBGP routers (any port).

7. Deny and log any other connections to or from BGP port 179.

Sample rules are given below:

```
permit tcp <IBGP router>/32 <EBGP router>/32 any 179
permit tcp <IBGP router>/32 <EBGP router>/32 179 any
... repeat as needed for other IBGP routers
permit tcp <EBGP router>/32 <EBGP router>/32 any 179
permit tcp <EBGP router>/32 <EBGP router>/32 179 any
... repeat as needed for other EBGP routers
permit tcp <IBGP router>/32 <IBGP router>/32 any 179
permit tcp <IBGP router>/32 <IBGP router>/32 179 any
... repeat as needed for other IBGP routers

deny tcp any any 179 179 log
```

4.2.5 Peripheral Traffic Filtering

Internet service providers can eliminate most forms of source address spoofing by implementing filters that reject traffic from a downstream network with a source address other than known prefixes. The following example is provided in BCP 38 (RFC 2827) [35]:

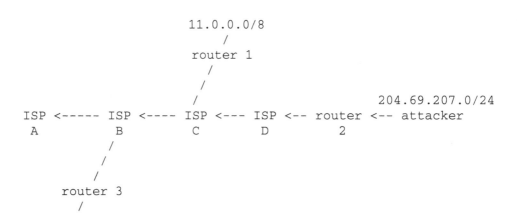

`12.0.0.0/8`

ISP D's router #2 serves addresses originating within 204.69.207.0/24 only, so rejecting traffic with a source address outside of this range will eliminate a large proportion of possible source spoofing-based attacks. An attacker within the downstream network would be able to forge another address within 204.69.207.0/24, but not from, for example, 204.69.209.0. However, by limiting the number of actual possible sources, post-attack investigation will be much easier. In the event that a prolonged attack on the network requires cutting off a range of addresses, fewer innocent users will experience disruption. Installation of similar filtering rules in all of the ISP's routers provides a reasonably strong control at minimal cost. Some practical considerations for implementing filtering capabilities are discussed in [54].

4.2.6 Reverse Path Source Address Validation

One option for eliminating forged packets is to check routes to a packet's source address, using the router's forwarding information base (FIB) to ensure that the return path would use the same interface as that where the packet was received. This method of validation has become less practical over time, as network growth has increased the prevalence of asymmetric routing. This method may thus be practical at edge interfaces for an ISP, but of limited use elsewhere. RFC 3704 [40]describes methods to reduce problems with reverse path-based validation.

4.3 Sequence Number Randomization

Because packet-based networks allow packets to take a variety of paths through the network, some messages may be received in a different order than they were sent. TCP, over which BGP is transported, uses sequence numbers to ensure that packets are assembled into the correct order by the receiving system. On establishing a connection (Figure 4-1), the systems at either end of the connection exchange an Initial Sequence Number that should be selected at random from a range of 32-bit integers. The sequence number is incremented with each message, making it possible to determine the correct order in which to reassemble packets, which comprise pieces of a message. The receiving system will accept packets that are within a configurable window around the sequence number for the session. Packets outside of the window are assumed to be in error (e.g., possibly duplicated or late), and are discarded.

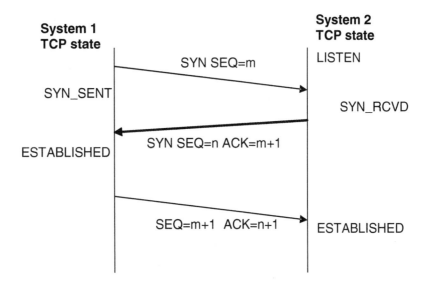

Figure 4-1. TCP Sequence Number Establishment

Sequence numbers were designed to allow for reassembly of messages and protect against transmission errors. They also provide a minimal protection against session hijacking and message spoofing (see Section 3.2.3) because an attacker must be able to predict the correct sequence number for a session to fool the victim system into accepting the forged packet as legitimate. Ideally, initial sequence numbers should be chosen at random, so that an attacker has a probability of only 2^{32} of guessing the correct number. Unfortunately, many operating systems and network devices have flawed algorithms that do not provide good initial sequence number randomization [8], [66], making it possible for a sophisticated attacker to forge messages for session hijacking or spoofing. The risk of these attacks can be reduced by ensuring that vendor patches for sequence number algorithms are up to date. Stronger defense is provided by using IPsec to fully protect TCP and BGP messages.

4.4 Generalized TTL Security Mechanism (TTL Hack)

The Time to Live (TTL), or "hop count", field is an 8-bit field in each IP packet that prevents packets from circulating endlessly in the Internet. At each network node, the TTL is decremented by one, and is discarded when it is reduced to zero without reaching its destination (see Figure 4-2). The TTL serves a variety of purposes for Internet protocols, since it provides a count of the number of nodes through which a packet has passed, simply by subtracting its current value from its initial value. As the Internet has grown, the number of nodes through which a packet may pass has increased. It is not unusual for 20 or more hops to be required before a packet is finally received, so a packet that starts with a value lower than this has a high probability of being discarded before it reaches its intended destination. For normal communication, a TTL initial value of 64 is typically used.

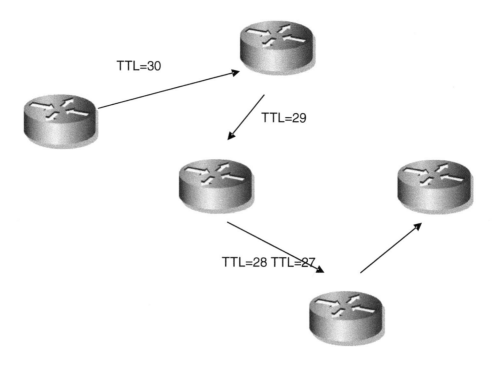

Figure 4-2. TTL Processing

The Generalized TTL Security Mechanism (GTSM, RFC 3682 [39]), often referred to as the "TTL hack", is a simple but effective defense that takes advantage of TTL processing. As noted, normal communications such as e-mail or Web browsing often require 20 or more nodes to reach their destination, and this value varies depending on the application. With BGP, however, peers are normally adjacent, thus only one hop should be required for a packet sent in a BGP message. A BGP message that has passed through multiple nodes is therefore almost certainly either an error or a packet from an attacker. The TTL hack sets the TTL to 255 on outgoing packets. Since routers decrement the TTL field by one when a packet is forwarded, adjacent peers should see incoming packets with TTL = 255. (Note that some implementations decrement the TTL before processing, in which case the incoming packets should have TTL = 254.) A lower value is an indication that the packet originated from somewhere other than the neighboring peer router (see Fig. 4-3). (Note that it is impossible for the packet to start with an initial value above 255, because the TTL field is an 8-bit value.) When implementing the TTL hack, it is also possible to set an expected incoming value below 255 on a per-peer basis when the peer is a known number of hops away, allowing a small variation to allow for changes in topology. For example, if the peer is known to be one hop away, the adjacent peer should reject packets with a TTL < 254. One limitation with the TTL hack is its availability. Code implementing RFC 3682 is provided on newer routers from major vendors, but may not always be included on older, or "legacy", routers, so not all organizations may be able to deploy it.

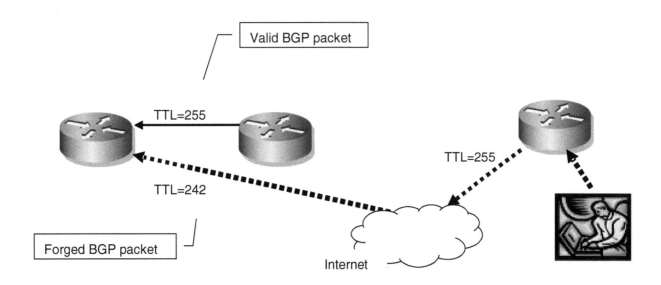

Figure 4-3. BGP TTL Hack

4.5   MD5 Signature Option

The MD5 hash algorithm (RFC 2385 [31]) can be used to protect BGP sessions by creating a keyed hash for TCP message authentication. MD5 takes a variable length message and computes a fixed length "digest", a 128-bit cryptographic hash (checksum) value, for each packet using a secret key that is shared by both ends of the session. Because MD5 is a cryptographic algorithm, rather than a simple checksum such as CRC32, it is computationally difficult to determine the MD5 key from the hash value. MD5 is designed so that a single bit change to a packet will produce a different hash value, so the receiving peer can be reasonably certain that no changes, deletions, or insertions have been made to BGP messages. BGP peers can include an MD5 value with each message, and the receiving peer checks to ensure that the value matches that computed using the shared secret key. If the values do not match, or the MD5 checksum is missing, the message is discarded.

RFC 2385 includes the following caution: "This document defines a weak but currently practiced security mechanism for BGP. It is anticipated that future work will provide different stronger mechanisms for dealing with these issues." In theory, approximately $\sqrt{2^{128}} = 2^{64}$ operations should be needed to find a collision (to be able to modify the message without detection) in a 128-bit hash. NIST has never endorsed MD5, judging it insufficiently secure for many uses. Weaknesses in MD5 were discovered in 1995, and it was fully broken in 2004, but despite its weaknesses MD5 is available in many routers and can provide significantly better security than no authentication for BGP.

MD5 provides protection against TCP-based attacks such as spoofing and session hijacking, because the attacker must know the secret key used in the hash computation. Commercial routers offer MD5 as a configuration option, and it is relatively easy to set up, using one or two statements in configuration files. A disadvantage is that a secret key must be shared between every pair of peers, and the keys must be updated periodically to prevent brute force cracking by an attacker who has accumulated a large volume of messages. In a large operation this can be expensive and time-consuming. An additional consideration is that, because MD5 uses a shared secret key, keys must be changed at the same time by both ends of the BGP connection, so administrative errors can result in disruption to routing operations. Because password crackers are widely available, which can also be used for cracking keys, strong keys should be chosen. See the key selection and management guidelines in RFC 3562 [38].

4.6 IPsec

In evaluating the security of a BGP configuration, it is important to keep in mind that BGP is transported over the standard TCP protocol. While randomized sequence numbers and the TTL hack can make an attacker's job more difficult, they are not cryptographically secure. Whenever an attacker has access to unencrypted traffic between BGP peers, these systems are vulnerable to a variety of TCP-based attacks, such as peer spoofing and session hijacking. The only comprehensive solution to these vulnerabilities is a cryptographic protocol such as IPsec.

IPsec is an IP layer protocol, so standard BGP can use IPsec without modification. IPsec can provide both authentication and data encryption (see RFC 4301 [45]), and thus could be used instead of MD5 authentication. Where only authentication is needed, the Authentication Header (AH) option can be used at the IP layer. An added layer of protection is available using the Encapsulating Security Payload (ESP) option to encrypt the data passed in BGP updates. Alternatively, IPsec tunneling can provide encryption of BGP data. The principal disadvantage of IPsec is the need to coordinate keys with BGP peers, as with MD5. Additionally, the strong encryption used with IPsec can be resource-intensive, adding processing load to routers that may be already close to overload. In most cases, encryption of BGP data should not be needed, since the information is expected to be passed throughout the Internet anyway, so using only cryptographic authentication (IPsec or MD5) may be the most cost-effective approach to adding security.

4.7   BGP Protocol Variations and Configuration

BGP implementations vary in their handling of protocol events, and some configuration changes can affect how events are handled as well. Some investigations (e.g., [14]) suggest better BGP security or dependability with some protocol variations, as described below. It is not clear that these options are always preferred, but administrators should review the following list and evaluate whether the findings are relevant to their system and configuration.

Table 4-1. BGP Event Handling

Event	Behavior found preferable in testing
SYN from non-configured peer	Drop silently
Spoofed SYN from configured peer	Reject with RST-ACK or SYN-ACK
OPEN from non-configured peer	Reject with RST or error
OPEN from configured peer with invalid AS number or ID	Reject with error
SYN flood	Do not allow progress past SYN_RECVD
OPEN	Initial sequence number randomization
OPEN	Source port randomization
Connection failures	Provide configurable logging of connection failures
UPDATE transmission	Implement BGP TTL hack
MD5 and TCP processing sequence	Process MD5 after TCP validation checks to reduce processing load
Failed MD5 authentication from invalid peer, non-established session, invalid password	Drop silently instead of sending RST. This option reduces the impact on CPU load.

4.8   Router Protection and Physical Security

A basic part of securing BGP is protection of routers on which BGP is running. Procurement and operation of BGP routers should include at least the following:

Operate the router in a secure, locked room. Only authorized system administrators should have access. These restrictions reduce the potential for unauthorized physical access to the router, which would make compromise easy to accomplish.

To reduce the potential for denial of service attacks based on exhaustion of routing tables, configure routers with the maximum amount of memory affordable.

Provide an uninterruptible power supply (UPS) for all routers, to reduce the potential for router failure. In addition to fault tolerance considerations, a UPS reduces the chance of an attack on power supplies being used to crash routers and possibly lead to data loss or reset of passwords on restart.

Implement a software update policy to ensure that patches are incorporated into router software as soon as they are released by the router vendor and appropriately tested for suitability in the local environment. Keeping vendor-provided patches up to date is the most effective means of securing routers against unauthorized access, denial of service attacks, and other threats.

5. Recovery and Restart

BGP is an infrastructure protocol. That is, it is a service that is used to keep the Internet running, so a major risk to Internet operations from attacks on BGP is either local or widespread outage of service. Improving the dependability of systems subject to denial of service attacks can be done in two ways – increase the difficulty of an attack, or reduce the time needed to recover from such an attack. In availability terms, the first of these options corresponds to increasing system uptime, U, while attack recovery corresponds to reducing downtime, D (ignoring other sources of downtime). Availability is calculated as $U/(U + D)$. For example, a system with uptime of 1000 hours (over a measurement period) and a down time of 1 hour has availability of $1000/1001 = 99.9\%$. If recovery time can be reduced to 0.1 hours, availability improves significantly, to 99.99%. By contrast, if recovery time remains at 1 hour, defenses would have to be strengthened to hold off attacks for 10,000 hours to achieve the same 99.99% availability. So reducing the time needed to recover from a denial of service attack can improve BGP availability, and for some attacks may be a more cost-effective strategy than hardening defenses. (Note however that if a denial of service attack can be sustained, rapid recovery will not be sufficient.) Quicker recovery also means less disruption to other parts of the network.

5.1 Graceful Restart Mechanism for BGP

When a BGP router restarts, for any reason, its peer routers recognize that their sessions with this router went down and then back up, a sequence of events known as a single "route flap". They then clear all routes associated with the restarting router, send messages to other peers to withdraw routes learned from the restarting router, recompute BGP routes, generate routing updates to pass on to their peers, and regenerate their forwarding tables. When repeated, this behavior can place a heavy load on routers, degrading network operations. Vulnerabilities in router software that allow attackers to crash the router (or even force restart of BGP sessions) thus present an opportunity for denial of service attacks that can affect the network far beyond the restarting router.

Earlier in Sections 3.2.1, 3.2.2, and 3.2.4, we discussed TCP reset attacks and the possibility of triggering route flap damping (RFD). Repeated peering-session resets (either by means of TCP sequence number guessing, spoofed ICMP error messages, or via compromised routers) can cause extensive flapping and induce RFD penalty cutoffs in parts of the network. This can result in route withdrawals and unreachability in parts of the network. In [61], it was shown through simulations that RFD can help amplify the effect of peering-session attacks and contribute to unreachability durations that are ten times larger as compared to the case when RFD is not used. The problem is compounded if attackers try to exploit service providers' routing policies and topologically tune the peering-session attacks to maximize the extent and duration of unreachability. BGP graceful restart can help mitigate the effects of peering-session attacks.

BGP graceful restart [58] is designed to reduce the processing load associated with router restarts, making it possible for routers to restart without triggering a routing flap across the network. Graceful restart was designed as a reliability mechanism, but it can also reduce the impact of DoS attacks against BGP routers.

Under this protocol, a router advertises its graceful restart capability in its OPEN message for a new session. If both BGP peers support graceful restart, it will be used, otherwise they continue to operate according to standard BGP4. With graceful restart, when a router goes down and comes back up, a 'restart' bit is set to indicate that it has restarted. In addition, a forwarding flag is set to indicate that it has preserved its forwarding state, and thus peer routers do not need to recompute routes. As a result, peer routers receiving this update message do not pass on the restart to the rest of the network, by not withdrawing the routes they received from the restarting router. BGP graceful restart thus reduces unnecessary route withdrawals and recomputations. It works because the restarting router has preserved its forwarding state, allowing traffic to continue flowing as before the restart. If the restart has occurred because of a configuration change or other non state-preserving event, graceful restart is not used, to enable peer routers to notify the rest of the network of the need to recompute affected routes.

Figure 5-1 shows the graceful restart message sequence. The process is as follows:

1. When Router 1 starts its BGP session, it sends an OPEN message to Router 2, with flags set to indicate that Router 1 has graceful restart capability (code 64), and the protocols for which Router 1 can preserve its forwarding state (for example, IPv4).

2. If Router 2 also supports GR, it sends an OPEN message with GR capability flag set, and the protocols for which it can preserve forwarding state.

3. When Router 1 restarts, it reboots and continues to forward packets using its last known routing entries.

4. When Router 2 detects that the TCP session between it and Router 1 has dropped, it marks routes learned from Router 1 as STALE (routes learned from other routers are left alone). Router 2 also starts the restart_timer for Router 1. This timeout value is the maximum time that Router 2 will wait to receive a new OPEN message from Router 1. Router 2 continues to use paths learned from Router 1 while waiting for an OPEN to indicate that Router 1 has restarted. If a new OPEN is not received from Router 1 within the timeout period, Router 2 will remove all STALE routes (received from Router 1) that it had marked earlier and send updates/withdrawals to other peers.

5. When the OPEN is received, restart_timer is reset. At this point Router 2 starts the stalepath_timer.

6. After the session is re-established, Router 2 checks the Forwarding State in the OPEN message received from Router 1. If it is not set, Router 2 removes STALE routes that it had learned from Router 1 and recomputes its routing database.

7. Router 2 sends UPDATE messages to Router 1.

8. Router 1 waits for EOR messages from Router 2 and any other peers, then recomputes its routing information. Exception: if Router 2 or another peer of Router 1 had sent an OPEN message to Router 1 indicating that the peer was also restarting, Router 1 does not wait for the receipt of an EOR message from the restarting router. This condition prevents a deadlock in which both routers are waiting for EORs from each other.

9. Router 1 sends UPDATEs to Router 2, concluding with an EOR message. During this period, Router 2 checks stalepath_timer. If this timer expires the routes previously marked, STALE will be removed and the BGP process restarted.

10. Router 2 receives the EOR from Router 1, then any remaining STALE routes learned from Router 1 will be updated with new information or removed from the RIB and FIB databases. At this point, convergence is complete for Router 2.

While graceful restart is generally helpful in reducing network disruption that results from occasional faults or system maintenance, its effectiveness against malicious activity varies with a number of factors. Most critical is recovery time—that is, how quickly the router can reboot and send a BGP OPEN message after a failure. If the restart occurs before the restarting router's peers exhaust their timeout period, routing tables will experience minimal disruption. A second factor, out of the control of router operators, is the attack rate. If attackers can execute an attack sequence rapidly enough, they may be able to prevent the router from successfully restarting during the timeout period. Peers will then remove the routes they learned from the attacked router, and packet forwarding will be disrupted until the attack can be stopped and the BGP session restored, which may take a considerable amount of time.

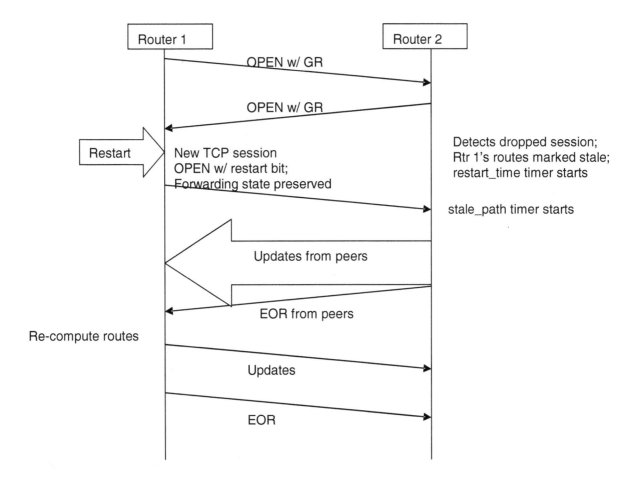

Figure 5-1. Graceful Restart Message Sequence

A plot from [61] is reproduced in Figure 5-2, which illustrates the probability of success that can be achieved by malicious attackers under some plausible scenarios of interest. The y-axis depicts the probability of RFD triggered isolation or withdrawal of prefixes, and the x-axis shows the rate of peering session attacks. The probability of success of an individual peering session attack is assumed as 0.1 (or, 10%). The plot illustrates that an attack rate at least two orders of magnitude higher is needed (i.e., much greater deterrence) to cause prefix withdrawals in the case of BGP with GR. From these results it appears that while RFD does have a flip side of aggravating the effect of peering session attacks, the adverse effect can be countered to some extent by the use of graceful restart for BGP. It may be noted that BGP-GR would still provide significant reduction of downtime in the event of attacks, even if use of RFD were discontinued as per a recent RIPE recommendation [60].

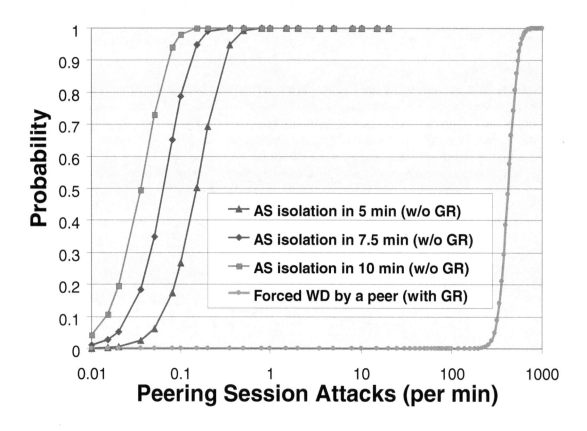

Figure 5-2. Attack Rates Needed to Cause RFD Triggered Isolation

5.2 Virtual Router Redundancy Protocol

The Virtual Router Redundancy Protocol (VRRP, RFC 3768, [42]) is designed to improve the reliability of routing protocols, including BGP, by providing one or more standby routers that can take over routing functions in the event that the primary router is disabled due to a failure or attack. With VRRP, a group of routers share an IP address. Collectively, the group is referred to as a "virtual router". One router is configured as the *master,* also referred to as the *IP address owner*, with others as *backups*. If the master fails, VRRP provides dynamic failover to one of the backup routers using an election protocol. In most cases, the transition to backup is accomplished within seconds, fast enough that no interruption occurs with the routing functions. VRRP can significantly reduce or eliminate "black hole" duration and speed recovery from failures, potentially including denial of service attacks.

Appendix A—References

[1]. Agarwal, S., C.N. Chuah, S. Bhattacharyya, C. Diot. "Impact of BGP Dynamics on Router CPU Utilization", Microsoft Research, http://research.microsoft.com/~sagarwal/pam04.pdf.

[2]. Barnes, R. and S. Kent, "An Infrastructure to Support Secure Internet Routing," Internet Draft, February 2007, http://tools.ietf.org/id/draft-ietf-sidr-arch-00.txt

[3]. Bellovin, S.M., and E.R. Gansner, "Using Link Cuts to Attack Internet Routing", AT&T Labs Research Technical Report. http://www.cs.columbia.edu/~smb/papers/reroute.pdf

[4]. Business Communications Review, March 2001. http://www.bcr.com/bcrmag/2001/03/p24.asp

[5]. CERT Advisory CA-2001-09, "Statistical Weaknesses in TCP/IP Initial Sequence Numbers," February 2005. http://www.cert.org/advisories/CA-2001-09.html

[6]. Chen, E., Y. Rekhter, "Outbound Route Filtering Capability for BGP-4", Internet Draft: http://www.ietf.org/internet-drafts/draft-ietf-idr-route-filter-16.txt

[7]. Christian, B., and T. Tauber, "BGP Security Requirements", draft-ietf-rpsec-bgpsecrec-07, Feb. 13, 2007. http://www.ietf.org/internet-drafts/draft-ietf-rpsec-bgpsecrec-07.txt

[8]. Cisco Systems, Cisco Security Advisory: "Cisco IOS Software TCP Initial Sequence Number Randomization Improvement". http://www.cisco.com/en/US/products/products_security_advisory09186a00800b1396.shtml

[9]. Cisco Systems, Cisco IOS Software: Beyond Basic IPVolume III, No. 19, THWARTING 'TCP-RESET' ATTACKS AT PUBLIC PEERING POINTS. http://www.cisco.com/warp/public/779/servpro/promotions/bbip/volume_03_issue19.html

[10]. Cisco Systems, BGP4 Case Studies/Tutorial Section 1. http://www.ittc.ku.edu/EECS/EECS_800.ira/bgp_tutorial/13.html#A1.0

[11]. Cisco Systems, BGPv4 Security Essentials Version 0.5. http://www.nanog.org/mtg-0206/ppt/BGP-Risk-Assesment-v.5.pdf

[12]. Cisco Systems, "Strategies to Protect Against Distributed Denial of Service (DDoS) Attacks," Document ID 13634, http://www.cisco.com/warp/public/707/newsflash.html

[13]. Convery, S., M. Franz, and D. Cook, "An Attack Tree for the Border Gateway Protocol," draft-ietf-rpsec-bgpattack-02, January 6, 2007, http://tools.ietf.org/wg/rpsec/draft-ietf-rpsec-bgpattack/

[14]. Convery, S., and M. Franz, "BGP Vulnerability Testing: Separating Fact from FUD v1.1", http://www.nanog.org/mtg-0306/pdf/ciag-bgp-v1-1.pdf

[15]. Eddy, W. TCP SYN Flooding Attacks and Common Mitigations, draft-ietf-tcpm-syn-flood-01. http://www.ietf.org/internet-drafts/draft-ietf-tcpm-syn-flood-01.txt

[16]. Farley, T., P. McDaniel, and K. Butler, "A Survey of BGP Security Issues and Solutions". http://www.patrickmcdaniel.org/pubs/td-5ugj33.pdf

[17]. Fuller, V., "Scaling issues with routing and multihoming," presentation at the IRTF Routing Research Group meeting, Prague, Czech Republic, March 2007. http://www.vaf.net/~vaf/apricot-plenary.pdf

[18]. Gont, F, "ICMP attacks against TCP", draft-ietf-tcpm-icmp-attacks-01.txt, October 2006. http://www.gont.com.ar/drafts/icmp-attacks-against-tcp.html

[19]. Huston, G., "Analyzing the Internet BGP Routing Table", The Internet Protocol Journal, March 2001.http://www.potaroo.net/papers/ipj/2001-v4-n1-bgp/bgp.pdf

[20]. Huston, G., BGP Routing Table Analysis Report, http://bgp.potaroo.net/as1221/bgp-active.html

[21]. Huston, G. and G. Armitage, "Projecting Future IPv4 Router Requirements from Trends in Dynamic BGP Behaviour," ATNAC 2006, http://www.potaroo.net/papers/phd/atnac-2006/bgp-atnac2006.pdf

[22]. IANA's Internet Protocol IPv4 Address Space, http://www.iana.org/assignments/ipv4-address-space

[23]. IETF, RFC 1518 – "An Architecture for IP Address Allocation with CIDR". http://www.faqs.org/rfcs/rfc1518.html

[24]. IETF, RFC 1519 – "Classless Interdomain Routing (CIDR): an Address Assignment and Aggregation Strategy". http://www.faqs.org/rfcs/rfc1519.html

[25]. IETF, RFC 1771 – "A Border Gateway Protocol 4 (BGP-4)". http://www.faqs.org/rfcs/rfc1771.html

[26]. IETF, RFC 1772 – "Application of the Border Gateway Protocol in the Internet". http://www.faqs.org/rfcs/rfc1772.html

[27]. IETF, RFC 1930 – "Guidelines for creation, selection, and registration of an Autonomous System (AS)". http://www.faqs.org/rfcs/rfc1930.html

[28]. IETF, RFC 1997 – "BGP Communities Attribute". http://www.faqs.org/rfcs/rfc1997.html

[29]. IETF, RFC 2270 – "Using a Dedicated AS for Sites Homed to a Single Provider". http://www.faqs.org/rfcs/rfc2270.html

[30].   IETF, RFC 2283 – "Multiprotocol Extensions for BGP-4".
       http://www.faqs.org/rfcs/rfc2283.html

[31].   IETF, RFC 2385 – "Protection of BGP Sessions via the TCP MD5 Signature
       Option". http://www.faqs.org/rfcs/rfc2385.html

[32].   IETF, RFC 2439 – "BGP Route Flap Damping".
       http://www.faqs.org/rfcs/rfc2439.html

[33].   IETF, RFC 2545 – "Use of BGP-4 Multiprotocol Extensions for IPv6 Inter-
       Domain Routing". http://www.faqs.org/rfcs/rfc2545.html

[34].   IETF, RFC 2796 – "BGP Route Reflection: An Alternative to Full-Mesh IBGP",
       updates RFC 1966. http://www.faqs.org/rfcs/rfc2796.html

[35].   IETF, RFC 2827 (BCP 38) – "Network Ingress Filtering: Defeating Denial of
       Service Attacks which Employ IP Source Address Spoofing".
       http://www.faqs.org/rfcs/rfc2827.html

[36].   IETF, RFC 2918 – "Route Refresh Capability for BGP-4", September, 2000.
       http://www.ietf.org/rfc/rfc2918.txt

[37].   IETF, RFC 3065 – "Autonomous System Confederations for BGP".
       http://www.faqs.org/rfcs/rfc3065.html

[38].   IETF RFC 3562, "Key Management Considerations for the TCP MD5 Signature
       Option," July 2003. http://tools.ietf.org/html/rfc3562

[39].   IETF, RFC 3682 – "Generalized TTL Security Mechanism (GTSM)".
       http://www.faqs.org/rfcs/rfc3682.html

[40].   IETF, RFC 3704 – "Ingress Filtering for Multihomed Networks", March 2004.
       http://www.ietf.org/rfc/rfc3704.txt

[41].   IETF, RFC 3765 – "NOPEER Community for Border Gateway Protocol (BGP)
       Route Scope Control". http://rfc.sunsite.dk/rfc/rfc3765.html

[42].   IETF, RFC 3768 – "Virtual Router Redundancy Protocol (VRRP)".
       http://www.ietf.org/rfc/rfc3768.txt

[43].   IETF RFC 4271, "A Border Gateway Protocol 5 (BGP-4)", January 2006,
       (obsoletes RFC 1771).
       http://www.rfc-editor.org/rfc/rfc4271.txt

[44].   IETF, RFC 4272, "BGP Security Vulnerabilities Analysis", January 2006.
       http://www.ietf.org/rfc/rfc4272.txt

[45].   IETF RFC 4301 – "Security Architecture for the Internet Protocol," December
       2005, (obsoletes RFC 2401), also see companion RFCs 4302-4309,
       http://www.rfc-editor.org/rfc/rfc4301.txt

[46]. IETF, RFC 4456 – "BGP Route Reflection: An Alternative to Full-Mesh IBGP". http://www.faqs.org/rfcs/rfc1966.html

[47]. Karlin, J., S. Forrest, and J. Rexford, "Pretty Good BGP: Improving BGP by Cautiously Adopting Routes," in Proc. IEEE International Conference on Network Protocols, November 2006.

[48]. Leiden, K., J. Keller, and J. French, "Context of Human Error in Commercial Aviation", National Aeronautics and Space Administration, Ames Research Center, December 2001.

[49]. Manning, B., "Documenting Special Use IPv4 Address Blocks that have been Registered with IANA." http://www.isi.edu/~bmanning/dsua.html

[50]. Manning, B., "Documenting Special Use IPv4 Address Blocks". https://datatracker.ietf.org/public/idindex.cgi?command=id_detail&id=3889

[51]. Mao, Z.M. R. Govindan, G. Varghese, and R.H. Katz, "Route Flap Damping Exacerbates Internet Routing Convergence," Proceedings of ACM SIGCOMM, Pittsburgh, PA, August 2002, pp. 221-233.

[52]. NISCC Best Practices Guide – Border Gateway Protocol, April 2004. http://www.cpni.gov.uk/docs/re-20040401-00392.pdf

[53]. NISCC Vulnerability Advisory 532967 – Vulnerability Issues in ICMP packets with TCP payloads, December 2005, http://www.cpni.gov.uk/docs/re-20050412-00303.pdf

[54]. Morrow, C., G. Jones, and V. Manral, "Filtering Capabilities for IP Network Infrastructure". http://tools.ietf.org/pdf/draft-ietf-opsec-filter-caps-05.pdf

[55]. Patel, K. "ASpath Based outbound Route Filter for BGP-4", Internet Draft: http://www.ietf.org/internet-drafts/draft-ietf-idr-aspath-orf-09.txt

[56]. Ramaian, A., R. Stewart, M. Dalal, "Improving TCP's Robustness to Blind In-Window Attacks", draft-ietf-tcpm-tcpsecure-07.txt http://www.ietf.org/internet-drafts/draft-ietf-tcpm-tcpsecure-07.txt

[57]. RIPE-229 - RIPE Routing-WG, "Recommendations for Coordinated Route-flap Damping Parameters," Version 2.0, October 2001 (obsoleted by RIPE-378). http://www.ripe.net/docs/ripe-229.html

[58]. Sangli, S., Y. Rekhter, R. Fernando, J.G. Scudder, and E. Chen, "Graceful Restart Mechanism for BGP". http://www.ietf.org/Internet-drafts/draft-ietf-idr-restart-10.txt

[59]. Smith, P., and C. Panigl, "Recommendations on Route-flap Damping", RIPE Routing Working Group, RIPE-378 (obsoletes RIPE-229, RIPE-210, RIPE-178),

11 May 2006. ftp://ftp.ripe.net/ripe/docs/ripe-378.txt

[60].   Smith, P., R. Evans, M. Hughes, "RIPE Routing Working Group
         Recommendations on Route Aggregation", RIPE-399, Dec. 2006
         ftp://ftp.ripe.net/ripe/docs/ripe-399.pdf

[61].   Sriram, K., D. Montgomery, O. Borchert, O. Kim, and R. Kuhn, "Study of BGP
         Peering Session Attacks and Their Impacts on Routing Performance," *IEEE
         Journal on Selected Areas in Communications*: *Special issue on Network Security*,
         Vol. 24, No. 10, October 2006, pp. 1901-1915.
         http://www.antd.nist.gov/pubs/Sriram_BGP_IEEE_JSAC.pdf

[62].   Team-Cymru Bogon List, http://www.cymru.com/Documents/bogon-list.html

[63].   Thomas, R., Secure BGP Template.
         http://www.cymru.com/Documents/secure-bgp-template.html

[64].   Touch, J., "Defending TCP Against Spoofing Attacks", draft-ietf-tcpm-tcp-
         antispoof-06.txt, Feb. 2007,
         http://www.ietf.org/internet-drafts/draft-ietf-tcpm-tcp-antispoof-06.txt

[65].   Woodcock, B. and G.R. Upadhaya, "Internet Exchange Point Tutorial," SANOG
         VIII, August 2006.

[66].   Zalewski, M., "Strange Attractors and TCP/IP Sequence Number Analysis".
         http://www.bindview.com/Support/RAZOR/Papers/2001/tcpseq.cfm

Appendix B—Acronyms

Selected acronyms used in the publication are defined below.

AH	Authentication Header
APNIC	Asia Pacific Network Information Centre
AS	Autonomous System
ASN	Autonomous System Number
BCP	Best Current Practice
BGP	Border Gateway Protocol
BGP-4	Border Gateway Protocol 4
CIDR	Classless Interdomain Routing
DHCP	Dynamic Host Configuration Protocol
DNS	Domain Name System
EBGP	Exterior Border Gateway Protocol
ESP	Encapsulating Security Payload
FIB	Forwarding Information Base
FISMA	Federal Information Security Management Act
GR	Graceful Restart
GTSM	Generalized TTL Security Mechanism
IANA	Internet Assigned Number Authority
IBGP	Internal Border Gateway Protocol
ICANN	Internet Corporation for Assigned Names and Numbers
ICMP	Internet Control Message Protocol
IETF	Internet Engineering Task Force
IGP	Interior Gateway Protocol (e.g., iBGP, OSPF, RIP)
IP	Internet Protocol
IPsec	Internet Protocol Security
IPv4	Internet Protocol version 4
IPv6	Internet Protocol version 6
ISP	Internet Service Provider
IT	Information Technology
ITL	Information Technology Laboratory
LAN	Local Area Network
MED	Multi-Exit Discriminator
NAT	Network Address Translation
NIST	National Institute of Standards and Technology
OMB	Office of Management and Budget
OSPF	Open Shortest Path First

RFC	Request for Comments
RFD	Route Flap Damping
RIB	Routing Information Base
RIP	Routing Information Protocol
SNMP	Simple Network Management Protocol
TCP	Transmission Control Protocol
TCP/IP	Transmission Control Protocol/Internet Protocol
TTL	Time to Live
UPS	Uninterruptable Power Supply
VOIP	Voice Over Internet Protocol
VRRP	Virtual Router Redundancy Protocol

Appendix C—Definitions

Selected terms used in the publication are defined below.

adj-RIB-In: Routes learned from inbound update messages from BGP peers.

adj-RIB-Out: Routes that the BGP router will advertise, based on its local policy, to its peers.

Aggregate: To combine several more-specific prefixes into a less-specific prefix.

Autonomous System (AS): One or more routers under a single administration operating the same routing policy.

Autonomous System Number (ASN): A two-byte number that identifies an AS.

BGP Peer: A router running the BGP protocol that has an established BGP session active.

BGP Session: A TCP session in which both ends are operating BGP and have successfully processed an OPEN message from the other end.

BGP Speaker: Any router running the BGP protocol.

EBGP: A BGP operation communicating routing information between two or more ASes.

Flapping: A situation in which BGP sessions are repeatedly dropped and restarted, normally as a result of line or router problems.

Generalized TTL Security Mechanism (GTSM): A configuration in which BGP peers set the TTL value to 255 as a means of preventing forged packets from distant attackers.

IBGP: A BGP operation communicating routing information within an AS.

loc-RIB: Routes selected from the adj-RIB-In table.

Multi-Exit Discriminator (MED): A BGP attribute used on external links to indicate preferred entry or exit points (among many) for an AS.

Appendix D—BGP State Transitions

State	Event	Actions	Message	Next State
Idle	BGP Start	Initialize resources Start ConnectRetry timer Initiate a transport connection	none	Connect
	others none none			Idle
Connect	BGP Start	none	none	Connect
	Transport connection open	Complete initialization Clear ConnectRetry timer	OPEN OpenSent	
	Transport connection open failed	Restart ConnectRetry timer	none	Active
	ConnectRetry timer expired	Restart ConnectRetry timer Initiate a transport connection	none Connect	
	others Release	resources	none	Idle
Active	BGP Start	none	none	Active
	Transport connection open	Complete initialization Clear ConnectRetry timer	OPEN OpenSent	
	Transport connection open failed	Close connection Restart ConnectRetry timer	none Active	
	ConnectRetry timer expired	Restart ConnectRetry timer Initiate a transport connection	none Connect	
	others none none			Idle
OpenSent	BGP Start	none	none	OpenSent
	Transport connection closed	Close transport connection Restart ConnectRetry timer		
	Transport fatal error	Release resources	none	Idle
	Receive OPEN message	Process OPEN is OK	KEEPALIVE	OpenConfirm
		Process OPEN failed	NOTIFICATION	Idle
	others	Close transport connection Release resources	NOTIFICATION Idle	
OpenConfirm	BGP Start	none	none	OpenConfirm
	Transport connection closed	Release resources	none	Idle
	Transport fatal error	Release resources	none	Idle
	KeepAlive timer expired	Restart KeepAlive timer	KEEPALIVE	OpenConfirm
	Receive KEEPALIVE message	Complete initialization Restart Hold Timer	none Established	
	Receive NOTIFICATION message	Close transport connection Release resources	none Idle	
	others	Close transport connection Release resources	NOTIFICATION Idle	
Established	BGP Start	none	none	Established
	Transport connection closed	Release resources	none	Idle
	Transport fatal error	Release resources	none	Idle
	KeepAlive timer expired	Restart KeepAlive timer	KEEPALIVE Established	
	Receive KEEPALIVE message	Restart Hold Timer	KEEPALIVE	Established
	Receive UPDATE message	Process UPDATE is OK	UPDATE	Established
	Receive UPDATE message	Process UPDATE failed	NOTIFICATION	Idle
	Receive NOTIFICATION message	Close transport connection Release resources	none Idle	
	others	Close transport connection Release resources	NOTIFICATION Idle